Foreword

God did not give mankind a complete revelation of His being and His will in the early years of history. Instead, He gave many bits of revelation each of which set forth a portion of truth only (Heb. 1:1). God also spoke in various ways, these ways being various men through whom the Word was given, such men as Moses and Joshua and Job. It was no accident that the Book of Job was the earliest part of God's written Word. It has been a source of encouragement, comfort and enlightenment for God's people over the last four thousand years.

A word of explanation is in order concerning the use of the *Amplified Version* in the poetic portion of Job which begins in 3:1 and ends in 42:6. This translation is widely accepted in Bible-believing circles, and throws some very revealing light on portions of Job which have been somewhat obscure to the average reader.

Where the *King James Version* is used in Job, it is identified by the letters KJV. It is also used almost without exception in the quotations from the other parts of the Old Testament and the New.

The messages which follow provide us with a very practical exposition of the Book of Job. They were first given over the special international network of the Back to the Bible Broadcast.

—The Publishers

Contents

CHAPTER ONE

A MAN CALLED JOB

The Book of Job is probably the oldest of the Bible books. It was written before the giving of the Law, a fact not hard to see. It would have been impossible in a discussion covering the whole field of sin, of the providential government of God, and of man's relationship to God without reference to the Law if the Law had been known. The time of writing was at least 1500 and perhaps as much as 2000 years before Christ.

Most of the original Book was written in poetic form. The first two chapters, which constitute the introduction, are in prose. Beginning with the third chapter and continuing on through 42:6 the form is poetical. From 42:7 to the end of the chapter it is prose, providing a few historical facts concerning Job's later life.

The subject matter is of great importance for our spiritual lives. This has been summarized in various ways. Someone has suggested that the Book speaks of the mystery of suffering, but this is too large a field. Actually the Book deals with a specific type of suffering. It answers the question: Why do the godly suffer? In the course of exploring this subject we see the experience of a righteous man in learning deliverance from himself.

One Bible teacher has summarized the message of the Book of Job in the following question: "Can I serve

God simply for who He is and not for what I get from Him for myself?" This type of inquiry is heart-searching. Do we serve God for self-interest or for His interest? We will see later how Job met this test.

We cannot fail to see in the study of the Book of Job that there is always a divine purpose in the believer's suffering. God never allows us to suffer needlessly. It will help us to see this in the case of Job and then to apply the truth to our own lives. This was a lesson Job himself had to learn, but it took time for him to learn it.

If I were to give a title to this series of studies I would call it: "A Man Who Had to Die to Live." Our Lord said, according to John 12:24,25: "Except a corn of wheat fall into the ground and die, it abideth alone: but if it die, it bringeth forth much fruit. He that loveth his life shall lose it; and he that hateth his life in this world shall keep it unto life eternal." This is a truth that is well developed in this ancient portion of the Scriptures.

Job Described

In brief but pointed phrases Job is described in the first verse in the Book. "There was a man in the land of Uz, whose name was Job; and that man was perfect and upright, and one that feared God, and eschewed evil." Four statements are made here about Job and these four statements summarize his qualities as a man in the eyes of God.

First of all he is said to be "perfect." This word does not mean sinless perfection but that Job was wholeheartedly given over to pleasing God. There was deep and true sincerity in this. He was single-minded, not double-minded. He was a man of integrity, not seeking to serve two masters but one, and that Master was God. Job had riches. He worked for them and worked to increase them but not in order to have them for himself. He was wealthy because

JOB, A MAN TRIED AS GOLD

or

A Man Who Had to Die to Live

By THEODORE H. EPP
Founder and Director
of
Back to the Bible Broadcast

A
BACK TO THE BIBLE
PUBLICATION

Back to the Bible

Lincoln, Nebraska 68501

50,000 printed to date—1976
(5-5257—4M—46)
ISBN 0-8474-1293-8

Grateful acknowledgement is made to Zondervan Publishing House, Grand Rapids, Michigan for permission to use the Amplified Version *in portions quoted from Job 3:1 through 42:6, the poetic section of the Book.* The Amplified Old Testament, Part 2, *copyright 1962, by Zondervan Publishing House.*

Printed in the United States of America

God blessed him; and one reason for his being blessed was his attitude toward the Lord.

Job is also described as an upright man. He had a good relationship with other human beings which was due to his having a right relationship with God. He was a man of unusual piety. Ezekiel speaks of him and places him on a level with two other outstanding Old Testament persons. The prophet said, "Though these three men, Noah, Daniel, and Job, were in it, they should deliver but their own souls by their righteousness, saith the Lord God" (Ezek. 14:14). James speaks of him in the New Testament and describes him as a man of great patience.

Incidentally, these same passages not only refer to the character of the man but they also establish his historicity. He was an actual person not a fictitious one. A grandson of Jacob was also named Job (Gen. 46:13), but is elsewhere known as Jasub (Num. 26:24; I Chron. 7:1). He was not the Job of the Book of Job.

Job was also a man who feared God. This in the Old Testament context means a man who had a reverential trust of God coupled with a hatred for evil. "The fear of the Lord," the Scriptures say, "is the beginning of wisdom," With that trust in God grows a sensitiveness to sin and a hatred of it.

In the fourth place Job was a man who eschewed evil, which means that he turned away from evil. He abstained from it and shunned it. His outward walk corresponded with his relationship with God.

We through trust in Jesus Christ have been cleansed from sin. Its guilt has been removed and we are counted righteous in God's eyes. We are born again, but does our conduct before men indicate what our relationship is before God? Job's conduct did. He was no hypocrite. He was a man of deep moral and spiritual character and God said of him: "There is none like him."

Job's Family and Possessions

Verses two through four tell us about Job's children and what his wealth consisted of. He had seven sons and three daughters. He owned seven thousand sheep, three thousand camels, five hundred yoke of oxen, five hundred she asses, and a very great household. The Scripture adds: "This man was the greatest of all the men of the east" (v. 3).

It is evident from the Book that Job was a man of considerable culture. He was a ruler respected by those around him, and he was familiar with history, astronomy and science in general. With all of this he had a very real spiritual heritage.

Job was a man greatly concerned for his family. We are told that his sons "went and feasted in their houses, every one his day; and sent and called for their three sisters to eat and to drink with them. And it was so, when the days of their feasting were gone about, that Job sent and sanctified them, and rose up early in the morning, and offered burnt-offerings according to the number of them all: for Job said, "It may be that my sons have sinned, and cursed God in their hearts. Thus did Job continually" (vv. 4,5).

There is no mention of the Law in this passage and yet Job knew about the need for making sacrifices. This was a truth that had been passed down from the days of Adam. God saw to it that men knew these things. Job as a faithful prophet and priest for his family was careful to obey. He was what we would call in New Testament language "a born-again" man of God. He knew the value of intercession and met his responsibility in that area.

Job's Need

In recognizing all of these things we still must come back to the fact that Job was not sinlessly perfect. His natural self was tainted as is ours. There was a root of evil in his heart that had to be laid bare. He belonged to the family of God; he was deeply in earnest in his devotion to God; and he was upright and departed from anything that he knew to be evil. Nevertheless, he did not know the depth of his own depravity. He did not know the truth that Paul expressed so clearly in Romans 7:18 where he said, "For I know that in me (that is, in my flesh,) dwelleth no good thing."

In spite of Job's devotion to the Lord his conscience still needed to be made more sensitive to sin. He needed to be instructed more clearly in orde: to understand what God knew about his heart. The testings that would come would do a refining work in his life and bring him to a knowledge of himself such as he did not have before the testings began.

The twelfth chapter of Hebrews deals with this subject. It shows that God is not satisfied merely to save us but that He also wants us to grow into the likeness of Christ. This is why the Lord permits chastening. Here are the words: "And ye have forgotten the exhortation which speaketh unto you as unto children, My son, despise not thou the chastening of the Lord, nor faint when thou art rebuked of him. . . . Now no chastening for the present seemeth to be joyous, but grievous: nevertheless afterward it yieldeth the peaceable fruit of righteousness unto them which are exercised thereby" (vv. 5,11).

Before God brought this to a happy conclusion in Job's life, the patriarch had a highly commendable self-image. His evaluation of himself is found in chapter 29: "Oh, that I were as in the months of old, as in the days when God watched over me; When His lamp shone above and upon my head, and by His light I walked through darkness; As I was in the (prime) ripeness of my days, when the friendship and counsel of God were over my tent; When the Almighty was yet with me, and my children were about me; When my steps [through rich pasturage] were washed with butter, and the rock poured out for me streams of oil! When I went out to the gate of the city, when I prepared my seat in the street—the broad place [for the council at the city's gate]; The young men saw me, and hid themselves; the aged rose up and stood; The princes refrained from talking, and laid their hand on their mouth; The voice of the nobles was hushed, and their tongue cleaved to the roof of their mouth.

"For when the ear heard, it called me happy and blessed me; and when the eye saw it, it testified for me —approving; Because I delivered the poor who cried, the fatherless and him who had none to help him. The blessing of him who was about to perish came upon me, and I caused the widow's heart to sing for joy. I put on righteousness, and it clothed me and clothed itself with me; my justice was like a robe and a turban, a diadem or a crown! I was eyes to the blind, and feet was I to the lame. I was a father to the poor and needy, the cause of him I did not know I searched out. And I broke the jaws or the big teeth of the unrighteous, and plucked the prey out of his teeth . . . Men listened to me and waited, and kept silence for my counsel. After I spoke they did not speak again, and my speech dropped upon them [like a refreshing shower]" (vv. 2-17,21,22).

This was how Job saw himself, but he needed God's evaluation, for Job could not see deep enough into his own heart.

Job's knowledge of himself needed to be brought into line with God's knowledge of his heart. God has given us His Book to help us see this truth. We see it in Job, but if we miss the lesson for ourselves, we miss much else besides. There is a knowledge of Christ that goes far beyond the mere historical record of His life. Paul said in Philippians 3:10: "That I may know him, and the power of his resurrection, and the fellowship of his sufferings, being made conformable unto his death." To know God in His holiness and perfection of His purpose was something Job needed and something we need.

Job did not come to this position easily. Good man though he was, he had pride that he did not recognize at first. He was bewildered with the treatment he received from men and even children who used to honor him. He thought he had been forsaken by God. Perhaps we have passed through a similar situation in which we have asked ourselves just why God was punishing us. It was likely that He was not punishing us at all. He allows these things to come so that we might have a new evaluation of Him and of ourselves.

Job had to find out how hollow and fickle this world is; and the same was true of his lower nature. As long as Job had plenty, the world was his friend. But many persons forsook him when he was stripped of his possessions.

The fickleness of people is illustrated time and again in the Bible. It is even illustrated in the life of our Saviour. On one day the crowd was singing praises to God and blessing Him who came in the name of the Lord. They sang thus believing that Christ was going to become their King. But when He refused (He will become King at His second coming), they turned against Him. So it was not long before the same crowd was crying: "Crucify him, crucify him!"

Man under control of the natural self is not to be trusted. All is well when the sun shines, but when the freezing blasts of winter arrive the story is different.

As long as the prodigal son had money to spend and lived a riotous life, he had many friends. But one day his money was all gone and so were his friends. We read: "And when he had spent all, there arose . . . famine . . . and he began to be in want. And he went and joined himself to a citizen of that country; and he sent him into his fields to feed swine" (Luke 15:14,15).

He had fallen so low that he would gladly have eaten the food furnished for the swine but no man gave it to him. It is right here that the Scripture adds these words: "And when he came to himself." This is what he needed to do, and this is what eventually took place in Job's life though he was not a prodigal. This is what we need to do when we are in the midst of testing. It does not mean that we have to get away from God as the prodigal did from his father; but if we will turn our situation over to the Lord, we will see things in their proper light.

This was true of Job. When he came into the presence of the Lord, the egotism revealed in chapter 29 and the bitterness expressed in chaper 30 all disappeared.

The general design of this Book is to justify the ways of God with men. God is just and what He does is right. His ways with men are never wrong. They are always correct. This is a truth that will become very clear as certain misconceptions which arise from man's imperfect knowledge of God are removed from our minds.

A number of years ago I was in a motel in an out-of-the-way place. I like to pick such a spot for a weekend when I have, what I call, a spiritual retreat. I do this several times a year.

I was at one of these places facing some great problems which related to myself and to the work. I did not know what to do, and one night I could not sleep. I finally got up and began to read the Scriptures. It came to me in a new way that what I needed was to have a new understanding of God. I opened my Bible to this Book of Job and read the last few chapters. Then I dropped on my knees and poured out my heart to God. It was about 3 o'clock in the morning when God met me in a new way, and things began to happen that changed the whole order of life for me and for the work. We all need such meetings with God.

Job's Flashes of Insight

We need to realize that there is a benevolent purpose of God behind all the sufferings endured by His people. Life's bitterest experiences have God's gracious purposes back of them. Job saw this according to the 23rd chapter. In spite of all his suffering he acknowledged that God's purposes were always good. Job had his problems but he did not lose his faith in God. He had some severe trials and went through deep waters, but every once in a while he came out with some outstanding statement concerning God that blessed him then and helps us now.

In verse 8 of chapter 23 Job said, "Behold, I go forward and to the east, but He is not there; or backward and to the west, but I cannot perceive Him; On the left hand and to the north, where He works [I seek him], but I cannot behold Him; He turns Himself to the right hand and the south, but I cannot see Him." Then Job made this remarkable and heartwarming statement: "But He knows the way that I take—He has concern for it, appreciates and pays attention to it. When He has tried me, I shall come forth as refined gold [pure and luminous]."

Can we trust ourselves into the hands of God? Are we confident that He seeks only the best for our lives? The Psalmist made reference to this when he said, "For thou, O God, hast proved us: thou hast tried us, as silver is tried. Thou broughtest us into the net; thou laidest affliction upon our loins. Thou hast caused men to ride over our heads; we went through fire and through water: but thou broughtest us out into a wealthy place. I will go into thy house with burnt-offerings: I will pay thee my vows, Which my lips have uttered, and my mouth hast spoken, when I was in trouble" (Ps. 66:10-14).

Here was a man who was in trouble but God brought him out of it. Not only that, God brought him into a place that he would not have enjoyed except for his trials.

The same truth is given in Romans 8:28,29: "And we know that all things work together for good to them that love God, to them who are the called according to his purpose. For whom he did foreknow, he also did predestinate to be conformed to the image of his Son, that he might be the firstborn among many brethren." The purpose God is working toward is to make us conform to the image of His Son, Jesus Christ.

Peter dealt with the same general line of truth. He wrote: "Beloved, think it not strange concerning the fiery trial which is to try you, as though some strange thing happened unto you: but rejoice, inasmuch as ye are partakers of Christ's sufferings; that, when his glory shall be revealed, ye may be glad also with exceeding joy" (I Pet. 4:12,13). Then he adds in the 14th verse: "If ye be reproached for the name of Christ, happy are ye; for the spirit of glory and of God resteth upon you: on their part he is evil spoken of, but on your part he is glorified." Let us then allow God to glorify Himself in and through our suffering. This was true in Job's case and can be in ours, also.

CHAPTER TWO

A PEEP BEHIND THE SCENES

In the first two chapters of the Book of Job, God gives us a peep behind the scenes so that we can see events on earth from the standpoint of heaven. There is no doubt that if Job could have seen into the councils of heaven before and during his trial, he would have answered his friends quite differently. But God did not allow him to know about this heavenly scene presented to us. Nor did God explain it to him at the close of his experiences. He may have learned about it after he went to heaven but not before.

God has permitted us to see these things to help strengthen our faith when baffling afflictions come upon us. His purpose is that we might place implicit faith in His counsel and goal, believing that the hard experiences in life are permitted for a good purpose. This is the teaching of Romans 8:28,29: "All things work together for good" for the believer. We are given this look behind the scene so that we will realize there is a blessing awaiting us if we suffer willingly and submissively under the hand of God.

This is no isolated subject of God's Word. We read in I Peter 5:10: "But the God of all grace, who hath called us unto his eternal glory by Christ Jesus, after that ye have suffered awhile, make you perfect [mature], stablish, strengthen, settle you."

God's eternal purpose for Job would have been thwarted if Job had been given the explanation for his trial. Had he known all that went on behind the scenes in heaven there would have been no place for faith. Without faith, Hebrews 11:6 tells us, it is impossible to please God. Job could never have come forth purified as gold is purified in the fire if he had not had to go through the situation in which he simply had to learn to trust God implicitly. Neither can we get anything from God apart from faith in Him. There are things which God cannot reveal to us at present; we must trust Him for the answer. Perhaps we are passing through some serious testings. There are serious trials showing up in our lives. Yet God does not reveal to us what His ultimate purposes are in these things, but He does teach us through them to have confidence in Him. If He were to prematurely reveal His reasons for allowing specific trials to come to us, there would be little or no room for faith to function. Faith in God and His Word and His eternal purposes is basic to receiving blessing from His hands.

There is a sense in which it is easy to believe God when we are healthy and strong. I personally have not had a serious illness. I do not know what it is to suffer like some Christians suffer. Yet illness is not the only trial that comes to us. I have had to face testings with regard to this ministry and to leadership in it that others could not possibly experience because they are not in the same situation.

Regardless, however, of what our trials consist of, the principle laid down in Hebrews 12 holds true: "Now no chastening for the present seemeth to be joyous, but grievous; nevertheless afterward it yieldeth the peaceable fruit of righteousness unto them which are exercised thereby. Wherefore lift up the hands which hang down, and the feeble knees; And make straight paths for your feet, lest that which is lame be turned out of the way; but let it rather be healed." This passage teaches us among other things that we should not complain when passing through testing. There will be those who see us, and if they hear us complain, will say, "If that is a Christian, I don't want to be one." We are to make straight paths so that those persons who observe us will want to be what we are. They will want to have what we have when they see us facing life's troubles as God intended us to. Others will want the same grace and strength in their lives that they see in ours.

The passage in Hebrews continues: "Follow peace with all men, and holiness, without which no man shall see the Lord: Looking diligently lest any man fail of the grace of God; lest any root of bitterness springing up trouble you, and thereby many be defiled" (Heb. 12:14,15). God has an abundance of grace for all the testings we meet. There is no cause for us to become bitter; but if we do, we give way to something that defiles many others. Our bitterness will contaminate them.

Faith is the basis for God's working in us. He reveals enough to us to make faith intelligent; but He also withholds enough to give faith complete scope for development.

Present Suffering and Future Glory

The Book of Job does not discuss the whole subject of suffering. It does not take up, for example, the suffering of those who do not know the Lord. People often say in their unbelief: "If there's a God in heaven, why does He allow all the suffering we see around us in the world today?" The Book of Job does not explain this phase of God's government. It does explain why the godly suffer. It also provides encouragement for the believer in the midst of any specific suffering even though he does not know what the goal of that particular trial is. But that trial, with all the others God permits to come into our lives, helps bring us to spiritual maturity. We will, undoubtedly, have questions concerning the future and the eternal results connected with our suffering, but we will keep on trusting God. This is sufficient for us, and it pleases Him when we show faith.

We reach a happy condition in the Christian life when we acknowledge that God knows what He is doing. A passage bearing on this is I Peter 4:13: "But rejoice, inasmuch as ye are partakers of Christ's sufferings; that, when his glory shall be revealed, ye may be glad also with exceeding joy." When the Lord returns, He will bring His rewards with Him. That day will be a day of exceeding joy for us. All of God's purposes in allowing suffering to come to us are not realized in the immediate present.

Another related passage is II Timothy 2:12: "If we suffer, we shall also reign with him." There is sufficient information here for us to know that a wonderful future lies before the believer who allows suffering to have its perfect work in his heart. This verse is in line with many others which promise us the privilege of reigning with Christ in His Millennial Kingdom.

This is suggested again in Romans 8:18: "For I reckon that the sufferings of this present time are not worthy to be compared with the glory which shall be revealed in us." Present suffering ensures future rewards. We may not understand all this, in fact, we do not; but we can believe God for it.

This truth is illustrated in the 13th chapter of Matthew. There the Lord tells how good seed is sown and then the Devil comes and sows bad seed. The two kinds of seed grow up together, but at the time of the kingdom "the Son of man shall send forth his angels, and they shall gather out of his kingdom all things that offend, and them which do iniquity; And shall cast them into a furnace of fire: there shall be wailing and gnashing of teeth. Then shall the righteous shine forth as the sun in the kingdom of their Father. Who hath ears to hear, let him hear" (Matt. 13:41-43).

The experience of the Lord Jesus Christ furnishes us with an excellent illustration of this also. We read in Hebrews 12:2 that we are to look unto Jesus the Author and

Finisher of our faith "who for the joy that was set before him endured the cross, despising the shame, and is set down at the right hand of the throne of God." The joy that was set before Him is elaborated on in Philippians. Christ was in the form of God but He thought it not robbery to be equal with God. He humbled Himself and became obedient unto death even the death of the cross. And the passage continues: "Wherefore God also hath highly exalted him, and given him a name which is above every name: That at the name of Jesus every knee should bow, of things in heaven, and things in earth, and things under the earth; And that every tongue should confess that Jesus Christ is Lord, to the glory of God the Father" (Phil. 2:9-11). Added to the thought of His being made preeminent is also the fact that through His death on the cross He provided for salvation for men. To see multitudes of individuals saved as the result of His sacrifice was part of that joy.

It is well to note that in the Book of Job which deals with the purpose of the suffering of the godly, such suffering is not imposed by a judge for wrongdoing on the part of the individual. Nevertheless it is suffering allowed to remedy something in the believer's life. It is not punishment, and yet it is designed to correct wrong. It is not retribution for wrong done, but discipline to refine the life to where the likeness of Christ becomes clear.

As Paul says in I Corinthians 13:12: "Now we see through a glass, darkly; but then face to face: now I know in part; but then shall I know even as also I am known." We do not grasp the significance of suffering now in its entirety; yet we know that there is blessing as a result of it. We are to learn to count ourselves dead to sin but alive to God. Self is to be refused and God is to be known. Can we learn to follow the Lord regardless of what we may get out of it for ourselves? We do not have to know why trials come. We just have to know that God is wise and knows what He is doing. This is good for the present life and for the life that is to come.

CHAPTER THREE

SATAN'S OPPOSITION

With regard to all trials and sufferings that come in a believer's life we need to keep in mind the truth of I Corinthians 10:13. There we are assured that God will not allow us to be tested beyond our ability but will with the testing make a way of escape. We need this assurance even more when we realize where some of the action against us lies and who our enemy is.

We learn in Job 1:6: "There was a day when the sons of God came to present themselves before the Lord, so Satan also came among them." The expression "sons of God" is used in two ways in the Scriptures. In the case before us it is speaking of angelic beings. But in other passages it deals with the children of God. In Genesis 6:2 where the phrase is found it has reference to the descendants of Seth, but in Job angels are meant.

Satan is not called a son of God. His name means "the accuser." In Revelation 12:10 he is called the "accuser of our brethren." Yet he has access to God for reasons best known to the Lord.

This is not an isolated truth in the Scriptures. We read in Zechariah 3:1,2: "And he showed me (Zechariah) Joshua the high priest standing before the angel of the Lord, and Satan standing at his right hand to resist him."

This function of Satan is clearly set forth in Luke 22:31,32. Our Lord said, "Simon, Simon, behold, Satan hath desired to have you, that he may sift you as wheat: but I have prayed for thee, that thy faith fail not: and when thou art converted, strengthen thy brethren." Peter was weak and Satan was going to sift him. This showed up later when Peter denied his Lord. This was the chaff in Peter which Satan was going to be used by God to remove. Satan was allowed to go only so far, for the Lord prayed for Peter that his faith would not fail.

Paul tells us in I Corinthians 5:5 of another power Satan has with regard to Christians. A believer in Corinth had committed such an outrageous sin that Paul said the church there was to deliver him "unto Satan for the destruction of the flesh, that the spirit may be saved in the day of the Lord Jesus." In heaven Satan is the accuser and on earth he is the destroyer. But, wherever he is, he is the enemy of God and of all that is good.

In Job 1:7 we read: "And the Lord said unto Satan, Whence comest thou? Then Satan answered the Lord, and said, From going to and fro in the earth, and from walking up and down in it." (KJV) This evil being is restless. He goes up and down in the earth but finds no place of peace.

Peter warns us of him when he says, "Be sober, be vigilant; because your adversary the devil, as a roaring lion, walketh about, seeking whom he may devour" (I Pet. 5:8).

Satan is a rebel prince of the earth, the spirit that now works in the sons of disobedience. He is called in Ephesians, "the god of this age." He is also "the prince of the power of the air." He binds and blinds wherever he can. He has many hosts of demons working under him: "For we wrestle not against flesh and blood, but against principalities, against powers, against the rulers of the darkness of this world, against spiritual wickedness in high places" (Eph. 6:12).

There are at least six things that we can learn from these verses in Job concerning Satan. We do not want to become centered in him, at the same time we dare not ignore him. We should know what his powers are and what his limitations are. Sometimes we attribute too much power to him and in some cases we attribute entirely too little.

Satan Accountable to God

First of all Satan is accountable to God. He came with the angels who presented themselves to give an account before God. The Accuser is also subject to divine authority. Though unwilling he still must report as do the others. His appearing before the throne is neither his privilege nor is it presumption. He is required of God to do this. He is compelled to stand before God and give an account of his conduct. Even though he is the arch rebel against God, he dare not evade this particular function. His activities are thus exposed before that dreadful throne of holiness. What a torture it must be for this evil being to have his activities constantly exposed in this way.

"And the Lord said unto Satan, Hast thou considered my servant Job, that there is none like him in the earth, a perfect and an upright man, one that feareth God, and escheweth evil?" (1:8). We realize from this that even the dark mind of Satan is an open book before God. God did not ask Satan this question because God did not know, but rather to draw out of Satan a confession of what was on his mind concerning Job. Perhaps a more accurate rendering of this passage would be: "Hast thou set thine heart on or against my servant Job, because there is none like unto him?"

Satan's Power Limited

Satan admitted that he had, but he also had to admit that he had been unsuccessful in doing anything against Job. Satan answered the Lord in this way: "Doth Job fear

God for nought? Hast not thou made an hedge about him, and about his house, and about all that he hath on every side? thou hast blessed the work of his hands, and his substance is increased in the land."

We can sing praises to God for He protects His saints. He has put a hedge around us. Satan cannot touch us unless God permits it. This is what the enemy of our souls admits in this very passage. This is the second fact we learn about Satan.

Satan Behind Evil in the Earth

We learn in the third place that Satan is behind the evil that curses the earth. God asked him where he had been, and his answer was that he had been up and down in the earth. What does he do in his journeyings? He is not only restless but he is evil and promotes ungodliness wherever he can. The Prophet Isaiah tells us: "But the wicked are like the troubled sea, when it cannot rest, whose waters cast up mire and dirt. There is no peace, saith my God, to the wicked" (Isa. 57:20,21).

We will never get very far in Christian work, particularly in soul winning, until we know how to deal with the one who binds and blinds the hearts of men. This is part of his evil work as he goes about in the world.

This is confirmed for us in II Corinthians 4:3,4: "But if our gospel be hid, it is hid to them that are lost. In whom the god of this world hath blinded the minds of them which believe not." Our business is to join with the Lord Jesus Christ in binding the strong man who is none other than Satan.

This is what Matthew tells us: "Or else how can one enter into a strong man's house, and spoil his goods, except he first bind the strong man? and then he will spoil his house. He that is not with me is against me; and he that gathereth not with me scattereth abroad" (12:29,30).

Satan Without Divine Powers

We also learn that Satan is not omnipresent. He can only be in one place at a time. He may move with lightning speed but he is localized, nevertheless. He cannot be everywhere at once. He cannot be putting pressure on every believer at the same time. We can praise God for this. However, Satan has hosts of demons that he uses and has organized for that kind of thing. This we have already seen from Ephesians 6:12.

Satan is not omniscient. He is not all-wise. God can read our minds but Satan cannot. Satan could not see clearly into Job's mind. He thought he could. He thought he knew what Job would do under certain circumstances but he was mistaken. Later on Satan was defeated.

There are occasions when Satan has taken possession of human minds as he did in the case of Judas. He cannot read your mind or mine, he only knows what we are thinking if we let it be known. He cannot force his way into these matters unless we permit him to. He does not have the power of God to be everywhere at the same time, neither does he have the wisdom of God to know all things. We dare not underrate this evil being, but neither should we overrate him.

Satan Is Under God's Control

The fifth lesson we learn about Satan in this passage is that he can do nothing without divine permission. Just as the waves of the ocean can come only so far, so it is with Satan. God permits him to go only so far but no farther. Someone has said that "Satan may be in the saddle but God is still on the throne." The Lord will not allow us to be tempted above that we are able but will with the temptation make a way of escape (I Cor. 10:13).

Satan Limited in Actions

In the sixth place, even though God gives Satan permission to do certain things He still places a definite limitation on Satan's actions. This is what we learn from Job 1:12: "And the Lord said unto Satan, Behold, all that he hath is in thy power; only upon himself put not forth thine hand. So Satan went forth from the presence of the Lord."

Satan could afflict Job but he could not touch his life. This was a lesson Pilate learned when he said to the Lord Jesus: "Why don't you answer me? Don't you know that I have power to crucify you, or to let you go?" Our Lord's answer was, "You have no power over me, except it were given to you from above."

According to I Corinthians 10:13 God always has His saints in mind. This is especially true in the time of trial. We are never out of His sight and never out of His mind. His heart of compassion goes out to us, so we need never think that Satan has been given the upper hand in our lives.

If we stay close to the Lord we never have to worry about what Satan may do. God gives us peace and victory and deliverance. Satan can only go so far but no farther. And God will give us strength and grace to meet whatever test Satan may throw in our way.

Satan the Slanderer

The Lord asked Satan, "Hast thou considered my servant Job, that there is none like him in the earth, a perfect and an upright man, one that feareth God, and escheweth evil?" Job, as we have seen, was a man who was wholeheartedly for God. He was truthful and dependable and reverenced God. At the same time he hated evil. He was considered one of the best-fitted men to be entrusted to withstand severe testing. God sometimes chooses such to be tried in the furnace of fire. But it is never without a purpose.

Satan's answer was, "Doth Job fear God for nought? Hast not thou made an hedge about him, and about his house, and about all that he hath on every side? thou hast blessed the work of his hands, and his substance is increased in the land" (v. 9,10). Satan is saying that it is no wonder Job is the kind of man he is, for God has hedged him in.

Satan suggests that Job fears God for a price. Who would not be faithful to a God who had blessed him as Job had been blessed? And so Satan answered: "But put forth thine hand now, and touch all that he hath, and he will curse thee to thy face" (v. 11).

This is bringing the matter down to what we considered previously. Can we serve God for what He is and not merely for what we get from Him?

In his slander Satan started with a certain amount of truth. But he went beyond that truth and assumed things that were wrong. This is a favorite technique of the Slanderer. And even we who know the Lord sometimes follow Satan's methods.

God alone knew Job's heart. God, of course, knew Satan's heart and mind also. We, like Satan, can only see from the outside. But sometimes we assume, as Satan did here, that we can know the hearts of others. Satan was wrong in Job's case, but he might have been right because there are many who worship God with their mouths though their hearts are far from him. The Lord looks on the heart and ponders it. He knows men as no other being can know them.

After David had committed his terrible sins he came in repentance before God and said, "For thou desirest not sacrifice; else would I give it: thou delightest not in burnt-offering" (Ps. 51:16). It is not the outward things that God was so concerned about. If the inward things were right, the outward actions would be right too. David said, "The sacrifices of God are a broken spirit: a broken and a contrite heart, O God, thou wilt not despise" (Ps. 51:17).

In another Psalm, David said, "Search me, O God, and know my heart: try me, and know my thoughts: And see if there be any wicked way in me, and lead me in the way everlasting" (139:23,24). David wanted God to check into his heart and see if there was any wrong worship, any injurious way that needed correcting. He placed himself before God and asked Him to look on the inside.

Men and the Devil can only look on the outside and draw conclusions from what they see. But since they cannot really know the heart, these conclusions can be and are often wrong. Satan could and did accuse Job. He could not attack Job's righteousness before God, but he did impugn Job's motives. This is a dangerous realm. Do you really know the motives of men, especially God's men?

Satan has no motives except that of selfishness and self-adulation. And apparently he thought that deep down in Job's heart he too had the same motives. All that was needed to prove this was to take down the hedge around Job and Job would be seen for what he really was.

In former days it was a common belief that goodness resulted in prosperity. Some persons still hold this idea. A good man is successful financially. He enjoys good health. He succeeds as a father. His family and his children share in his prosperity. Such a man possesses a kind of peace that men seek for. In fact, one of Job's visiting friends said, "Who that was innocent ever perished?"

People often measure the Back to the Bible Broadcast by its activities. Yet we have our financial testings; and when such times arise we usually check ourselves to find what we have done wrong. Then we are tempted to think that if everything is going well and the finances adequate this is proof of God's blessing upon us.

An opposite view of this is that some people think wickedness always issues in adversity. Many think they can measure a man or an institution as being in the will of God or not by their financial situation.

It would seem that Satan fosters this idea, but neither he nor any man can read another man's motives. If they can see adversity, they can only assume that some specific act of sin has been committed. Paul faced this kind of thing repeatedly and in answer to such an attitude he said, "For me, myself, it is of very little concern to me to be examined by you or any human court; in fact, I do not even examine myself. For although my conscience does not accuse me, yet, I am not entirely vindicated by that. It is the Lord Himself who must examine me. So you must stop forming any premature judgments, but wait until the Lord shall come again; for He will bring to light the secrets hidden in the dark and He will make known the motives of men's hearts, and the proper praise will be awarded each of us" (I Cor. 4:3-5, Wms.).

This then was Paul's answer to men who tried to judge his motives. But Satan who is the slanderer does not hesitate to slaughter reputations. He is a killer of good names. Some people join him in this sometimes in a harsh destructive way, and others do it under the guise of superior piety. Satan is efficient in every type of attack in this matter.

There are few persons who attend church any more regularly than does Satan. And he usually comes with subtle questions. His is not always an outright accusation. He said to God, for example: "Doth Job fear God for nought? Hast thou not made a hedge about him?" Questions are good in their place, but Satan used questions here to infer wrong on the part of Job.

Satan was sure that he was eminently qualified to examine men's hearts. He was a much-traveled person and had seen human nature under every circumstance in life. He thought he knew exactly what every man would do under certain circumstances. But assumptions are not proofs.

Take the case when Paul was seen in Jerusalem in

company with a Gentile. This was on a street in Jerusalem, a perfectly normal place for him to talk with a Gentile. Later, Paul was found in the temple alone, but his enemies assumed he had brought his Gentile friend with him into the temple court. They had no evidence to support their conclusion, but they sought Paul's life just the same. Had it not been for the Roman government intervening through its soldiers, Paul would have been murdered.

Satan still thinks he speaks with authority. He thinks he knows what a man is doing and why. However, Satan is a liar from the beginning, and he reads the worst into what men do. He thought he was perfectly safe in picking on Job in this way.

By asking questions he avoided the embarrassment of being faced with a lie for having stated something that was inaccurate. He reached his intended purpose by raising a question. But a question can be used to slander a man or a woman just as effectively as an outright accusation, sometimes even more so. But there is little risk of being charged with misrepresentation if a question is raised rather than an assertion made.

There is little comeback through a question of this nature. So where God commended Job, Satan brought insinuations that were intended to degrade Job. Methods such as these employed by Satan are not used by believers who truly love their brethren in Christ.

In that great love chapter in the Bible we read: "Love never boils with jealousy; It never boasts, is never puffed with pride; It does not act with rudeness, or insist upon its rights; It never gets provoked, it never harbors evil thoughts; Is never glad when wrong is done, But always glad when truth prevails" (I Cor. 13:4-6, Wms.).

D. L. Moody is credited with saying that a lie travels around the world before the truth can get its boots on. We may give praise to someone and say he is a good person; but then when we question his motives, we indirectly question his goodness. This is slander of a most subtle kind. Let us not unknowingly or knowingly become tools of Satan by destroying the good names of other believers.

Satan's Design in Slander

Why did Satan slander Job in this fashion? What was the Evil One driving at? The following from a book by C. G. Chapple exposes Satan's purposes quite thoroughly.

"It seems clear that he is seeking to disprove any goodness on the part of Job. While confessing every good deed that Job has done, he implies that all is vitiated by a false motive. Further, since Job, the best that God has to offer, is not a good man, there really is no good man at all. Since no man is good, there really is no such thing as goodness. Further still, this bad man, since he pretends to be good, is an outrageous hypocrite. Therefore, the very best that God and his saints have to offer is not only not good, he is the very worst of men.

"Now since there is no such thing as goodness, Satan is under no obligation to be good. That fact relieves him of all embarrassment.

"Satan is out to prove that there is no goodness and that such a thing as a good man is impossible.

"Now since Job, who claims to be the best of men, is in reality the worst of men, since he adds to his bad motives the ugly sin of hypocrisy, it follows that Satan is the better of the two. Satan does not claim any great merits for himself. He does not claim to fear God or to shun evil. He does not claim to have ever strengthened feeble knees or to have kept men on their feet or to have in any way ministered to the poor. But at least he has this in his favor: he has not pretended to such high deeds. He has been frank and open in his wickedness. At least he is not a hypocrite like Job.

"Here we see his cloven foot. Shrewd though he is, he is also quite stupid. In fact he is so stupid that he believes that he can build himself up by tearing somebody else down. He even foolishly persuades himself that the absence of the vice of hypocrisy guarantees the presence of virtue."

I believe this to be an accurate analysis of Satan's intentions. Let us now turn our attention to some other lessons from this same passage of Scripture.

Stay in God's Hedge

We should learn from chapter 1 of Job the need of staying within God's hedge. It was true that God had put a hedge around Job and all that he had. The Adversary is walking about seeking whom he may devour. He is out to reach those who may have stepped out from behind the hedge God has placed around them. Job, though he was attacked, stayed within the hedge and eventually triumphed.

I remember many years ago seeing a picture that left a distinct impression upon me. I have never come across it again. It was someone's drawing of Christ standing in the center of a large meadow. There was a fence around the meadow which enclosed many, many sheep. But there were small flocks of sheep outside the fence, removed from its protection. Pictured also, were demons trying to get sheep that were inside the meadow but close to the fence to join the flocks on the outside. I thought as I saw the picture that the closer we stay to Christ the farther we are from Satan.

Satan wanted God to remove the hedge. He said to the Lord: "But put forth thine hand now, and touch all that he hath, and he will curse thee to thy face" (v. 11). Satan was saying that God was claiming Job to be a good man but if the hedge were once removed Satan would prove Job was not good.

CHAPTER FOUR

SATAN'S SCHEMES

According to verse 12 the Lord gave Satan permission to afflict Job up to a certain point: "Behold, all that he hath is in thy power; only upon himself put not forth thine hand. So Satan went forth from the presence of the Lord."

God, knowing Job's heart, allowed Satan certain freedoms with Job. Are Satan's accusations true? Does good exist only in a pleasant environment? Is God afraid to let His children experience adversities? Is this why He keeps a hedge around this man Job? Can a person who knows and loves God be brought to the place where he renounces and curses Him? These are all questions which arise out of this bit of biographical material presented to us in the first chapter of Job.

God said to Satan that He would remove the hedge from around everything but Job's life. So, Satan went out to prove that Job was not what God claimed him to be; but God's purpose was to show that Job was a man of God.

At this point we must look again at I Corinthians 10:13. "God is faithful, who will not suffer you to be tempted above that ye are able; but will with the temptation also make a way of escape, that ye may be able to bear it." God does not promise that He will pull us away from a testing or trial but that He will give us His grace and power so that we can stand for Him in it. This was what God was going to do for Job. Not a hair of His child's head could fall without God's permission. God works out His purposes in us, so He may allow Satan to be the tool that He uses. Even Job, as good a man as he was, had to learn some real spiritual lessons. There was precious ore in his life that needed refining. Job saw this even in the midst of the trial, for he said, "But he knoweth the way that I take: when he hath tried me, I shall come forth as gold" (Job 23:10).

Satan lost no time in putting his plans into execution. Here is what we read: "And there came a messenger unto Job, and said, The oxen were plowing, and the asses feeding beside them: And the Sabeans fell upon them, and took them away; yea, they have slain the servants with the edge of the sword; and I only am escaped alone to tell thee" (vv. 14,15). Job's field hands and the animals needed for cultivating the soil were gone.

Hardly had this word been brought than he was given notice of another disaster: "While he was yet speaking, there came also another, and said, The fire of God is fallen from heaven [possibly speaking of lightning], and hath burned up the sheep, and the servants, and consumed them; and I only am escaped alone to tell thee" (v. 16). This was a serious blow to Job's finances.

Right on the heels of this disaster came another: "While he was yet speaking, there came also another, and said, The Chaldeans made out three bands, and fell upon the camels, and have carried them away, yea, and slain the servants with the edge of the sword; and I only am escaped alone to tell thee" (v. 17). The animals used in Job's commercial enterprises were now gone.

The worst blow of all came hard after these others: "While he was yet speaking, there came also another, and said, Thy sons and thy daughters were eating and drinking wine in their eldest brother's house: And, behold, there came a great wind from the wilderness [possibly something in the nature of a tornado], and smote the four corners of the house, and it fell upon the young men, and they are dead; and I only am escaped alone to tell thee" (vv. 18, 19). What a tremendous destruction of property and what remarkable powers in directing evil men and employing the forces of nature! Does Satan actually have such powers? We must remember that he was the chief of God's great angelic creation. He is Lucifer, the greatest creature ever created by God.

Various powers are accredited to this remarkable person. We learn in II Corinthians 4:4 that he has power over men's minds: "In whom the god of this world has blinded the minds of them which believe not." And in Ephesians 2:2 we read: "Wherein in time past you walked according to the course of this world, according to the prince of the power of the air, the spirit that now worketh in the children of disobedience." We learn from this that he influences men in the moral realm.

The world system is under Satan's control according to I John 5:19: "And we know that we are of God, and the whole world lieth in wickedness [the wicked one controls the world system]." Satan is also the instigator of lies among men. At one time our Lord found it necessary to say to the Scribes and Pharisees: "Ye are of your father the devil, and the lusts of your father ye will do. He was a murderer from the beginning, and abode not in the truth, because there is no truth in him. When he speaketh a lie, he speaketh of his own: for he is a liar, and the father of it."

Satan even has power in the realm of death. This is what we are told in Hebrews 2:14: "Forasmuch then as the children are partakers of flesh and blood, he also himself likewise took part of the same; that through death he might destroy him that had the power of death, that is, the devil." Christ's death on the cross brought to nothing Satan's power in death. This does not mean that Satan has the power to inflict death, for the wages of sin is death.

But Christ died in order to deliver them who "through fear of death were all their lifetime subject to bondage."

Satan has powers to impose bodily affliction. He has no creative power because all things were created by Christ and nothing was created apart from Him. But Satan is permitted certain powers over nature. This, however, is only by God's permission and with divine objectives in view.

When the great calamities fell upon Job it was not Satan's lightning nor Satan's whirlwind that brought destruction. The lightning and the wind belong to God. Satan had merely permission from God to use them. Even Job saw this for he said, "The Lord gave, and the Lord hath taken away; blessed be the name of the Lord."

Nevertheless, it was only by God's permission that Satan could do this. The Lord said, "Thou movedst me against him, to destroy him without cause."

These successive blows were brought right on the heels of each other. There was no chance for reflection or for recovery by Job before another blow fell. In three successive strokes he lost his wealth; and last of all, and most tragic of all, he lost his children.

Job's Response

Job's reaction was remarkable. Scripture says, "Then Job arose, and rent his mantle, and shaved his head, and fell down upon the ground, and worshipped" (v. 20). Then he said, "Naked came I out of my mother's womb, and naked shall I return thither: the Lord gave, and the Lord hath taken away; blessed be the name of the Lord" (v. 21). A divine comment is then made: "In all this Job sinned not, nor charged God foolishly" (v. 22).

The character of a man is generally revealed in an hour of sudden crisis. When there is no time for reflection, that which is in the heart will break out. This is especially true when someone is under such pressure as was Job. He knew nothing of the cloud of angelic witnesses who were looking on from heaven. They had been in on the conversation between God and Satan. They knew what was going to happen and were watching to see how this man of God would respond.

Job did a most remarkable thing for a man who had gone through what he had experienced. He worshipped. His soul was anchored in the Lord. He not only had a Saviour, but his Saviour was Lord and Master of his life. So, when his wealth and means of producing wealth were swept away and all his children lost to him, he worshipped God.

How would we react under such circumstances? Job was ready. All that Satan had thrown at him did not move him.

Satan was defeated by Job's turning to the Lord. The Evil One failed in everything he tried to do against Job. Instead of driving Job away from God, Satan had driven him closer to God. Here was a man who could be faced with all that Satan could cast at him and still stand, and having done all, stand.

Is this how we react when Satan brings trials and testings into our lives? Or do we cringe and ask why? Do we shake and tremble under the terrible trial as we see it breaking on us?

Job's words in which he said: "The Lord gave, and the Lord hath taken away; blessed be the name of the Lord" have a very special meaning in my life. We had our first-born son for nearly three years before God suddenly took him home. We loved the child, played with him, watched him develop, and then had to stand helplessly by when he fell ill. In a few hours he was gone.

When my father came, I said to him: "Dad, will you preach the funeral sermon? And please use this text: 'The Lord gave, and the Lord hath taken away; blessed be the name of the Lord.' " It was only by God's grace that my wife and I were able to respond in this way.

Satan's Second Attempt

But these events for Job were not ended at this point. There is much more. Once again we find the sons of God presenting themselves before the Lord and Satan among them. The Lord addressed Satan saying, "Hast thou considered my servant Job, that there is none like him in the earth, a perfect and an upright man, one that feareth God, and escheweth evil? and still he holdeth fast his integrity, although thou movedst me against him, to destroy him without cause" (2:3). God made it very plain here before Satan and before all the angels in heaven that there was no cause in Job for such calamities to befall him.

We, of course, see this now, for it is written for our learning. But Job did not see any of this.

Satan was not through. He said, "Skin for skin, yea, all that a man hath will he give for his life. But put forth thine hand now, and touch his bone and his flesh, and he will curse thee to thy face" (vv. 4,5).

Satan does not give up easily. He did not succeed the first time but he would try again. He had removed Job's possessions and his family, but now he was going to touch Job where he thought every man was vulnerable. Satan's proposition was now to add physical suffering to this man whom he thought was strained to the breaking point.

The Lord answered Satan and said, "He is in thine hand; but save his life" (v. 6). Again Satan was given permission to go so far but no farther. He could afflict Job's body but he could not take his life.

The record is, "So went Satan forth from the presence of the Lord, and smote Job with sore boils from the sole of his foot unto his crown. And he took him a potsherd to scrape himself withal; and he sat down among the ashes" (vv. 7,8).

God had given His permission so Satan brought a terrible disease on Job. Some think it was a form of black leprosy, the worst of all kinds of leprosy.

The very disease itself made Job an outcast. He went to the ash heap outside the city. There he was, the greatest man of the children of the East, yet he was compelled to take his place with beggars and outcasts. At one time he had sat in the gates of the city as the chief ruler among them. Now he sat upon an ash heap as the most despised among them. They looked down on him whom they once bowed to as their leading citizen. Will he keep his integrity under such circumstances?

Job's place outside the city reminds us of the experience of our own Saviour. We read of Him in Hebrews 13:12,13: "Wherefore Jesus also, that he might sanctify the people with his own blood, suffered without the gate. Let us go forth therefore unto him without the camp, bearing his reproach." We are told in the first part of that same chapter to "consider him that endured such contradiction of sinners against himself, lest ye be wearied and faint in your minds. Ye have not yet resisted unto blood, striving against sin." Jesus did strive against sin and resisted unto blood in order that we might be saved and that we might have grace after we were saved to stand against Satan's tests.

Satan's Third Try

Even after all this Satan was not through with Job. There was still another blow to come. His wife came to him and said, "Dost thou still retain thine integrity? curse God, and die" (v. 9). The last remaining member of his household, his own wife, forsook him. We would gather from her words that she advised Job to commit suicide. The one human being to whom he had the right to look for help and sympathy had now turned against him. His friends had forsaken him and he tells of it in the 30th chapter: "But now they that are younger than I have me in derision." Still in another place he said, "And now I am their song, yea, I am their byword. They abhor me, they flee far from me, and spare not to spit in my face. Because he hath loosed my cord, and afflicted me, they have also let loose the bridle before me." He meant by that that they had not held their tongues but had said anything before him they wanted to say. Then Job continued, "He hath cast me into the mire, and I am become like dust and ashes." This, then, was the situation which was made so much more grievous when his wife turned against him. The mother of his children no longer would stand by him.

This is an old strategy of Satan. He used it in the Garden of Eden. He deceived Eve and she fell and Adam with her. Satan's method was to question what God had said. In the case of Job's wife, Satan apparently induced her to question God's protection of His servant so that she concluded Job might as well die and get it over with.

A woman can make or break a man. I have lived long enough to see homes and businesses broken and Christian work destroyed because of some women. On the other hand, I have seen men rise to greater places of usefulness and effectiveness because of the help of a godly wife. And today a great deal of Christian work is done by godly women.

I was first a pastor of a church and now for nearly 30 years I have led this radio work. In several cases I have seen the worldly ambition of wives ruining their husbands. I personally know a number of ministers whose lives have been completely ruined in this way. They could not bring home enough money to satisfy the pleasures and benefits their wives desired.

On the other hand, I have seen men who could never have risen to the heights they did in usefulness to the Lord but for the love and sacrifice of their wives.

Job's wife had stood with him when he lost his wealth and his children and everything else that he had. After all, they were her children too. But now when he sat on the ash heap outside the city gate with people spitting upon him and mocking him and ridiculing him, it was too much for her. In her anguish and possibly misguided love she thought she would rather see him dead. She allowed Satan to borrow her mouth to question Job's integrity. It may have been love and pity for Job that brought her to this place; but if it was, she loved her husband more than she loved her God. Because of this she became the tool of Satan.

She must have thought that the God whom Job served had forsaken him. Possibly she thought God could not be a God of love since He had let such sufferings come upon a man who had served Him so well.

Is such an attitude not familiar to us? Have we not even thought these things ourselves?

So Job's wife asked him to renounce God and die. It was not a matter of Job dying eventually. She seemingly advocated suicide, a sort of "mercy killing" in this case.

Faithful and Unfaithful Wives

It is apparent from Scripture that many of the wives of the great men in the Bible did not live on the same spiritual plane as their husbands. Sarah was not a woman of faith to match Abraham's faith. God promised them a seed but as the years went by and no son was given them, she tried a human scheme that brought Ishmael into the world; but this was a tragedy. The people of Israel have been suffering from Sarah's suggestion and Abraham's falling in line with it ever since.

Then there was Zipporah. She was the wife of Moses but she balked at the thought of circumcising her sons. Moses was stricken with a serious disease because of the situation, and only when his sons were circumcised did he recover. She bitterly upbraided him for this.

Michal, the wife of David, was another. When David danced before the Lord for joy as the Ark was brought to the city, she mocked and ridiculed him. She apparently had no sympathy for his devotion to the Lord.

Faith is by necessity an individual matter. It is something between the soul and God. But what loneliness is present in family life when one of the partners to the marriage does not go as far as the other in submission and devotion to God.

It may be on the other hand, the husband who does not stand by his wife during her time of suffering. There are many faithful wives, and illustrations can be given from Scripture to show how in some cases it was the wife who was the person of faith in the family.

I thank God for the wife God has given me. Many times she has stood by in faith when I would have faltered had I been standing alone. Many a husband has been made an effective witness for Christ because his wife has encouraged him.

At one time in Luther's experience he came under so much criticism from his enemies that he became depressed. He wondered if it paid to suffer all he did for the sake of the truth. His wife realized the seriousness of the situation and determined with God's wisdom to do something about it. She put on a black dress, an expression of mourning, and went about her duties in the house.

Luther was startled at her appearance and asked her who had died.

"Oh," she said, "God did."

"God died? What do you mean?" he asked.

"Well," she said, "the way you've been acting God must be dead."

Her approach to his problem had the desired result. Thank God for faithful wives!

Satan must have thought he was dealing Job a last

crushing blow that would break down his defenses and the real Job would show through.

It was the real Job who reacted but a Job submissive to God. He said to his wife, "Thou speakest as one of the foolish women speaketh. What? Shall we receive good at the hand of God, and shall not we receive evil? In all this did not Job sin with his lips." Her attitude showed that she was willing to enjoy the good things God gave but was not willing to endure the hard times when they came. Job's wealth, his children, his friends, his servants, acquaintances and his health were all gone. But the final stroke against him lay in his wife's attitude. He was willing, however, to stand alone because his trust was in God.

Later on Job reasserted his faith in God when he said, "Though he slay me, yet will I trust in him: but I will maintain mine own ways before him" (13:15).

The following poem is one that I keep in my Bible, for it means a great deal to me:

Doth Satan sometimes buffet thee,
    And tempt thy soul to sin?
Do faith and hope and love grow weak?
    Are doubts and fears within?
Remember I was tempted thrice
    By this same foe of thine:
But he could not resist the Word,
    Nor conquer pow'r divine.

When thou art sad and tears fall fast
    My heart goes out to thee,
For I wept o'er Jerusalem—
    The place so dear to Me:
And when I came to Lazarus' tomb
    I wept—My heart was sore;
I'll comfort thee when thou dost weep,
    Till sorrows all are o'er.

Do hearts prove false when thine is true?
    I know the bitter dart;
I was betrayed by one I loved—
    I died of broken heart:
I loved My own, they loved Me not,
    My heart was lonely, too;
I'll never leave thee, child of Mine,
    My loving heart is true.

Have courage, then, My faithful one,
    I suffered all the way,
Thy sensitive and loving heart
    I understand today;
Whate'er thy grief, whate'er thy care
    Just bring it unto Me;
Yea, in thy day of trouble, call,
    And I will answer thee.

—Susanne C. Unlauf

CHAPTER FIVE

JOB'S COMFORTERS

We have seen how God pronounced Job to be a good man, upright, perfect, one who feared God and avoided evil. God said that there was no other man like him upon the earth. This does not mean, however, that Job was without an old nature, that perhaps his old nature had been eradicated. God allowed Job to be tested in such a way as to reveal that he did possess a fallen nature which was incurably evil. It was untamable; it could not be changed for the better. This is a nature all of us have. We inherited it from Adam.

In Romans 6 God reveals how the old nature or "old man," as it is sometimes called, is to be treated. We learn there that our "old man" was crucified with Christ. We are also told that we have been identified with Jesus Christ in His death; therefore, we are to count or reckon ourselves dead to the old nature or sin nature. What is true in our position before God, is to be counted as true in our daily experience. So then, God permitted Job to be tested in order to reveal to him that underneath all his goodness the old nature was still in evidence.

In my studies of Job, I have come to the conclusion that there is possibly no better way to expose the presence of the old nature than to do exactly what was done in the life of Job. He had heroically triumphed over all the tests Satan had thrown at him. He lost his property, his friends, his children; his health; and then his wife urged him to renounce God and die. But Job stood firm in the face of all of these calamities.

However, when his friends came, they accused him falsely. They insinuated things that were not true and attacked his motives. Possibly nothing will stir up the old man or old nature in us quicker than something like this. It is hard for us not to rebel when accused unjustly or an insinuation made about us that is absolutely untrue. This is especially so when we have tried to do what is right. Job was a benevolent person in every way, and he had been careful to avoid doing what he knew would displease God. So, to be accused of secret evil conduct and branded a hypocrite, aroused him to a spirited but carnal self-defence.

As I check my own life, I find that this is one place where Satan can get at me quicker than at any other place. It always takes some time for me to find the victory in a situation of this nature.

Apparently, this was the reason God allowed Job to face the unfair and stinging reproaches of his so-called friends. He could not take their charges. He knew they were wrong. He rebelled at the injustice of them, then went on to say things that later on he abhorred himself for. It was at this point he let the old nature control his life for a time.

There are certain deep-seated sins in the heart which are often hidden from the public eye under normal conditions of life and even under strains such as Job went through when he lost so much. But pride and the various aspects of self can still rise to the surface, though our tendency is to try to keep from being exposed. They belong to the life dominated by the old nature. It was not dead in Job but came to the fore. Thank God, when He had completed His work in Job's heart, the patriarch had a new understanding. First, he came to see the good purposes of God in dealing with him as He did. Second, he abhorred himself for the things he said and did when he allowed his fallen nature to creep to the front in his life.

So it was as Job sat alone, an outcast and seriously ill, that suddenly three men appeared on the scene. Here is the record: "Now when Job's three friends heard of all this evil that was come upon him, they came every one from his own place; Eliphaz the Temanite, and Bildad the Shuhite, and Zophar the Naamathite: for they had made an appointment together to come to mourn with him and to comfort him. And when they lifted up their eyes afar off, and knew him not, they lifted up their voice, and wept; and they rent every one his mantle, and sprinkled dust upon their heads toward heaven. So they sat down with him upon the ground seven days and seven nights, and none spake a word unto him: for they saw that his grief was very great" (Job 2:11-13).

Friends can be very valuable. The right kind of friends can help us over the difficult spots in life. But the quality of friendship expressed by these three men left much to be desired.

When they saw Job's plight they were flabbergasted. They hardly knew what to think. The man whom they had known as the greatest man in their part of the world was ill and sitting on an ash heap. They were silent for seven days, having no comfort to give him. They said nothing and apparently Job said nothing in all that time. But Satan kept up the pressure, and finally at the end of the seven days Job opened his mouth and cursed his day.

Consider some of the things he said: "After this Job opened his mouth, and cursed the day of his birth. And Job said, Let the day perish wherein I was born, and the night which announced, There is a man-child conceived. . . . Let the stars of the early dawn of that day be dark; let the morning look in vain for the light, nor let it behold the day's dawning. Because it shut not the doors of my mother's womb, nor hid sorrow and trouble from my eyes. Why was I not stillborn? Why did I not give up the ghost when my mother bore me? . . . For then should I have lain down and been quiet; I should have slept; then had I been at rest [in death], . . . Why is light [of life] given to him who is in misery, and life to the bitter in soul, Who long and wait for death, but it comes not, and dig for it more than hid treasures; Who rejoice exceedingly, and are elated when they find the grave? . . . For the thing which I greatly fear comes upon me, and that of which I am afraid befalls me" (Job 3:1-25).

What strange words from a man who had stood so nobly during the first terrible blows that befell him. He showed great faith in God. Then after a week of silence from his friends he seemed to lose his sense of personal worth. He felt he did not count any more. He was no longer an asset but a liability. He was a burden to himself and to everyone else. He thought life no longer had purpose or meaning.

In the wake of all these combined losses, now had come the crowning loss—faith that God cared. This was a most crucial moment in Job's experience. He cursed the day of his birth but he did not curse God. He forgot that God cared but he did not lose faith that God existed.

This was when his friends should have come to his help. This was when they should have encouraged him, but they did not.

What True Friends Are

Thinking about this matter made me interested in looking up the word "friend" in a Bible concordance. I found some very helpful things. For example, in Proverbs 27:5,6, I found this: "Open rebuke is better than secret love. Faithful are the wounds of a friend; but the kisses of an enemy are deceitful." A friend can be a real friend in a time of need if he will speak truth in the power of the Holy Spirit.

Again in Proverbs I read: "A friend loveth at all times, and a brother is born for adversity" (17:17). There is a very real purpose in having friends but there are times when, as Job found, he had no friends.

Another keen observation on the quality of human friendship is given in Proverbs 19:6: "Many will entreat the favor of the prince: and every man is a friend to him that giveth gifts." As long as Job had wealth he had many so-called friends. Now that everything had turned against him, his friends disappeared.

A formula for friendship is laid down in Proverbs 18:24: "A man that hath friends must shew himself friendly: and there is a friend that sticketh closer than a brother." A friendly person will gain friends. An unfriendly person will not. But thank God, there is one friend—a Divine Friend—who sticks closer than a brother. But even He found how fickle some friendships can be. David prophesied of it when he wrote concerning a deep hour of trial through which he was passing: "Yea, mine own familiar friend, in whom I trusted, which did eat of my bread, hath lifted up his heel against me" (Ps. 41:9).

Are we friends to those in need? Do we stand by fellow believers when they are in times of difficulty and stress? Or do we find someone on whom others are throwing mud and join in throwing mud with them?

Job needed a friend as never before. He thought God was standing aloof from him, watching to see if he had made a false step. As long as Job's suffering was outward and physical, he seemed to be able to stand up. But when doubts of God's goodness entered his mind he went down.

This is a crucial moment in all of our experiences. Satan will try to inject the thought that God does not care for us, proof of that being we have trials. This seems to be the first reaction of many of us when testings afflict us.

When any of us begin to doubt God's goodness, we

walk on very slippery ground. Paul avoided this by reminding himself of the truth he expressed in Romans 8:28:
"We know that all things work together for good to them
that love God, to them who are the called according to
his purpose."

While Job lost sight of God's goodness and cursed
the day that he was born, there were some treasures he
did not surrender. In spite of Satan's attacks, the final
one being the wrong views of Job's so-called friends, God
was still working and eventually Job was reclaimed. He
had many lessons to learn but he learned them because
he never lost his integrity. He could not be brainwashed
by his Adversary. Job never ceased to believe in the reality
of God even though he was tortured by many ugly thoughts
concerning the nature of God. Satan was eventually defeated and Job came through to greater victories than he
had ever enjoyed.

This is why God allows testings to come into our lives.
He wants to bring us into spiritual realms to which we
could never attain without the hard trials of life.

The attack Satan made on Job through the three so-
called friends who came to visit him was based on their
false ideas of piety. Yet Job never lost his integrity. This
has been defined as purity, moral soundness or honesty.
It is a quality that is free from corrupting influence or
practice. For the time being Job lost touch with God and
thought God was seeking to hide from him. Yet he did
not lose faith in the reality of God.

There have been others among God's people who have
faced similar situations but they seemed to have been
better prepared to meet them. Perhaps their remembering
Job's experience is the reason for that.

Paul's Victory

Paul came to a day when he found himself deserted
by men who should have been standing by him. He wrote

to Timothy: "At my first answer no man stood with me, but all men forsook me: I pray God that it may not be laid to their charge" (II Tim. 4:16).

This was an hour when Paul needed friends. He was in a dungeon in Rome for preaching the gospel. He had been falsely accused of wrongdoing and the day of his execution was drawing near. Nero was a cruel and unjust ruler and no reprieve could be expected from him.

Paul did not lose courage. He said, "Notwithstanding the Lord stood with me, and strengthened me; that by me the preaching might be fully known, and that all the Gentiles might hear: and I was delivered out of the mouth of the lion" (v. 17). But this was not all. Paul was triumphant, for he said, "And the Lord shall deliver me from every evil work, and will preserve me unto his heavenly kingdom: to whom be glory forever and ever. Amen." (v. 18). Paul was triumphant because he was prepared in advance for this situation.

Moments of Triumph

Job also had his moments of triumph even in the depths of his despair. Some of these statements we have already seen but another, an outstanding one, is given in Job 19:25-27. "For I know that my Redeemer and Vindicator lives, and at last—the Last One—He will stand upon the earth; And after my skin, even this body, has been destroyed, then from my flesh or without it I shall see God, Whom I, even I, shall see for myself and on my side! And my eyes shall behold Him, and not as a stranger! My heart pines away and is consumed within me."

Let us learn this lesson from Job's experience. He had his times of despair, but he came out victorious because God did not leave him. Job also had life from God and that life could not die. We who are trusting in Christ can also triumph for the same reasons in the midst of our troubles. Paul admonishes us in Galatians 6:9: "And let us not be weary in well doing: for in due season we shall reap, if we faint not." And Peter further encourages us with this thought: "But the God of all grace, who hath called us unto his eternal glory by Christ Jesus, after that ye have suffered a while, make you perfect, stablish, strengthen, settle you" (I Pet. 5:10).

To suffering Hebrew Christians in the early church, these words were written: "Cast not away therefore your confidence, which hath great recompense of reward. For ye have need of patience, that, after ye have done the will of God, ye might receive the promise" (Heb. 10:35,36). Do we believe God? Do we believe His Word? Are we willing to trust Him? These promises are given us in order to help us in the time of trial.

It will not hurt us to anticipate something of the triumph that Job enjoyed at a future time in his life. There came a day when he saw God for Himself. Job was brought to his knees and to the end of himself. He saw God as He really was, then great blessing followed. As we study the Bible we will find that all the men God used had an experience or experiences similar to this. Jacob met God at Peniel and came to the place where he put God first and himself last. He was never the same man again after that encounter with God.

Joshua met the Captain of the Host of the Lord. This meeting made all the difference in Joshua's life.

Isaiah tells in the sixth chapter of his prophecy how he saw God high and lifted up. This not only made a profound impression on the prophet but brought him into greater submission before God and prepared him for future service.

So we could go on speaking of Jeremiah and Ezekiel and Daniel in the Old Testament, and men such as Paul and the Apostle John in the New. They all met God face to face and were brought to the end of themselves. This was true of Job. We have said of him that he was a man who had to die in order to live. The doctrinal aspect of this is given in Romans 6, 7 and 8; but the practical aspect was a reality to Job long before that New Testament book was written.

A Brief Summary

It will be well to summarize some of these matters we have established before we consider in some detail the response of Job's three friends.

First of all, we must remember that God is deeply concerned about the welfare of His saints. Even though Job was not conscious of it, God had Job's best interests at heart and at no time deserted him.

Satan is an enemy who goes about seeking whom he may devour. He hates God and he hates all of God's children. He may at times appear as an angel of light in order to deceive us. He avoids showing himself in his true colors; instead, he employs one strategy or another to try and upset our spiritual balance.

God allows His children to be sifted. There is always a purpose behind this, however, and that purpose is the maturing of our spiritual lives.

We have also seen that Satan is used as a tool by God to sift the saints of God. Furthermore, Satan can go no farther than God allows him.

We would not say that Satan has patience, for this is a characteristic which comes from the Holy Spirit. But Satan is not one to give up. He is persistent. If he cannot overcome us in one way, he will try some other.

All of this emphasizes the fact that we need to be ready for any type of attack. We must be fortified. This is what Paul had reference to when he wrote: "Wherefore take unto you the whole armour of God, that ye may be able to withstand in the evil day." We do not know when this day may be, so we must be ready at all times.

We have also found that any doubt of God's motives or any thought that God does not care for us is a point of danger to us. Such thoughts lead us on to slippery ground.

Even when God's child fails, we can be sure that God is standing by and will not forsake His child. This should be an encouragement to us. The Psalmist saw this truth and stated: "The steps of a good man are ordered by the Lord: and he delighteth in his way. Though he fall, he shall not be utterly cast down: for the Lord upholdeth him with his hand" (Ps. 37:23,24).

Job's friends knew nothing of the heavenly scene that we have described for us in Job, chapters one and two, and of course, Job did not know about it either. The friends had another serious drawback in that they failed to understand the character of God. Furthermore, they knew nothing of the real object of His dealing with Job. This is true of most of us in a good many things of life. The Saviour said it for us when He said to Peter: "What I do thou knowest not now; but thou shalt know hereafter" (John 13:7). These things will not always be a mystery; some day we will understand.

In *Daily Bread* from the Radio Bible Class this truth is illustrated in the following story. A Dr. Pentecost was trying to comfort a woman who was passing through some sore trials. He picked up a piece of embroidery in which she had been working and said, "My, what a confusion of threads and colors. Why do you waste your time on a tangled mess like this?"

But the woman turned the embroidery over and said, "Look at it on this side. Isn't it beautiful? You were looking at it from the wrong side."

The Lord's servant then made the point that she was viewing her trials from the reverse side. If we are to see the benefits, we must look at them from God's side. He is working out a lovely design of His own choosing. When we get to heaven, we will see these things in their right perspective.

CHAPTER SIX

DISCOURSES OF THE COMFORTERS

Eliphaz

Job's three friends were undoubtedly great men, but in the 22 chapters that cover their discussions with him they did not produce an answer to his problems.

Consider now the first of these men whose name was Eliphaz. He was possibly the eldest of the group and supposedly the wisest also. However, superior age does not mean superior wisdom. The philosophy of Eliphaz was based on two things: the first of them we will call general observations, and the second, spiritual illumination. He claimed to have some kind of vision on which he laid a great deal of stress. Several times in the fourth chapter he stressed what he had seen and experienced.

There are people like this, especially in times of illness. When visiting a friend in a hospital, they will tell about their troubles and what they had gone through with physical difficulties. By sharing their experiences they may help. But the kind of experiences Eliphaz talked about were not of a helpful kind.

Eliphaz began his discourse by commending Job for his former piety. "Behold, you have instructed many, and you have strengthened the weak hands. Your words have held firm him who was falling, and you have strengthened the feeble knees. But now it is come upon you, and you faint and are grieved; it touches you, and you are troubled and dismayed . . . Think (earnestly), I beg of you; who that was innocent ever perished? Or where were those upright and in right standing with God cut off?" (Job 4:3-8).

Eliphaz used what is today called the psychological approach. One should commend before he condemns. We need to be alerted when somebody approaches with a flowery speech. We may have reason to wonder what they are going to criticize us for. Sometimes of course this is not the purpose.

Eliphaz then leaned heavily on his observations which were all related to his experience. No one, as far as he had seen, had ever perished being innocent. Suffering, according to his way of looking at it, was always the direct outcome of some specific sin. The suffering came as the result of God's judgment on sin. His conclusion was that Job was no exception to this rule and was being punished for some sin he had committed.

This is an idea that people have today. There are many persons who hold the position that if someone or some family passes through severe trials, such trials are deserved and result from specific wrongdoing.

If this were true, why was it David suffered as he did before he became king? He was hounded for his life not because he had done wrong but because Saul was jealous of him.

Jeremiah was thrown into a dungeon and treated like a common felon. Why? Simply because he preached the Word of God with boldness.

And what about our Saviour Himself. He did no wrong. In fact, He could do no wrong, yet He suffered.

It is easy to see that the argument of Eliphaz does not hold water.

In the next place Eliphaz gave his own pious reactions to what he would do if he were in a similar situation. How often people pass along such advice as this. They may have no concept at all of what another person is passing through, but they are sure they know what they would do under the circumstances. He said in 5:8: "As for me, I would seek God, inquiring of and requiring Him [as the breath of life] and to God would I commit my cause." But this was exactly what Job was trying to do though at first he seemingly could not find God.

Eliphaz knew something of the power of God in nature and expressed this point clearly. At the same time he injected some insinuations that Job could not fail to understand. "Who does great things and unsearchable, marvelous things without number; Who gives rain upon the earth, and sends waters upon the fields; So that He sets on high those who are lowly, and those who mourn He lifts to safety. He frustrates the devices of the crafty, so that their hands cannot perform their enterprise or anything of [lasting] worth. He catches the [so-called] wise in their own trickiness, and the counsel of the schemers is brought to a quick end" (5:9-13).

But what can a man do when God seems to be silent? There is a purpose even in this but Eliphaz did not recognize it.

The Scriptures tell us that God purifies our lives as the metalworker purifies silver. It is heated until the scum and dross rise to the top so that they can be ladled off. When the silversmith can see his image in the metal, he withdraws the heat. This is how God works in our lives. Through trials He purifies us.

Finally, Eliphaz began to summarize his first speech and said to Job: "Happy and fortunate is the man whom God reproves; so do not despise or reject the correction of the Almighty [subjecting you to trial and suffering]. For He wounds, but He binds up; He smites, but His hands heal" (vv. 17,18). Sometimes advice of this kind can be given too glibly. Whether it will be listened to depends on the condition of the other person's heart and mind.

Eliphaz then listed several things in which he said God will deliver His people. These are famine, war and scourge of the tongue, when one is afraid of destruction, the beasts of the earth, then a person will know that his seed will be great, and finally that he will come to his grace in full age like a shock of corn comes to its season.

In all the other arguments that Eliphaz used, for he made two further speeches, he made little progress. He did become more pointed in concluding Job to be a hypocrite. However, by calling Job a hypocrite, Eliphaz contradicted the first statements he made when he complimented Job.

The final appeal by Eliphaz is eloquent. Here are his words: "Acquaint now yourself with Him—agree with God and show yourself to be conformed to His will—and be at peace; by that you shall prosper and great good shall come to you. Receive, I pray you, the law instruction from His mouth, and lay up His words in your heart. If you return to the Almighty and submit and humble yourself before Him, you will be built up; if you put away unrighteousness far from your tents, If you lay gold in the dust, and the gold of Ophir among the stones of the brook [considering them of little worth], And make the Almighty your gold and the Lord your precious silver treasure, Then you will have delight in the Almighty, and you will lift up your face to God. You will make your prayer to Him, and He will hear you, and you will pay your vows" (22:21-27).

Job, who had been seeking God and had not as yet been able to find Him, hears this man telling him, "Just turn to God." There was no help from Eliphaz.

His proof for all of his philosophy was, "I have seen." But what one may experience and be true for him may not be true for someone else. To try to establish a general rule for all persons on the basis of one person's experience is a grave error. For example, one of the questions raised by Eliphaz was, "Who ever saw a righteous man suffer?" The fact is the righteous do suffer. The New Testament tells us that those who live godly in Christ Jesus shall suffer persecution. Illness, loss of goods and other trials have been the lot of many of God's children.

Eliphaz showed by his statements that he knew little of God's ways with men. He did not help Job and he does not help us today. There are many like him who claim special revelation and special experience. But the only safe ground for knowledge in these matters is the Word of God.

Bildad

Bildad was the second of the two friends who came to speak with Job. Like Eliphaz, Bildad had three discourses; these are found in chapters 8, 18 and 25. Eliphaz based his arguments largely on experience and particularly special revelation through a supernatural agency. Bildad, on the other hand, based his arguments on tradition. He went back to the fathers and to former ages for his authority. Here are his words: "For inquire, I pray you, of the former age, and apply yourself to that which their fathers have searched out; For we are but of yesterday, and know nothing, because our days upon earth are a shadow. Shall not the forefathers teach you, and tell you, and utter words out of their heart—the deepest part of their nature?" (8:8-10).

There is no appeal here to the revealed will of God but to whatever the wisdom might be that the fathers taught.

Bildad asked if God perverted judgment or justice? The answer, of course, is "no." Then Bildad used this premise to argue that Job must have lost his children because of some transgression on their part. He also charged Job with lack of purity and uprightness, else God would have listened to his plea.

This was little help to a man who, according to the first chapter of the Book, had been very careful in the rearing of his children. As the family priest Job had offered sacrifices to God just in case his children in their youthful exuberance or thoughtlessness had offended God in something they had said or done. Then to have them accused of some special sin which was so great that all of them had to give up their lives because of it was a terrible charge to make.

The arguments of Bildad were all from appearance and based on suppositions. He used many "ifs." He did not really know but he supposed many things. This was the way it looked to him. This was the way he interpreted the situation. But his interpretation was wrong. We as Christians need to learn to distinguish between facts and how the facts are interpreted. Just because we read something does not mean that we may insinuate that something else is also true. Just because someone interprets a set of facts in one way does not mean that interpretation is correct. All the facts may not be given in the report. And often the withholding of one essential fact can change the meaning of an event. This was Bildad's approach and it is a dangerous one.

He also appealed to what we call tradition. He said to inquire of the fathers, failing to state that the fathers may not all have agreed with each other. They may be scientists or philosophers or theologians and be at variance with each other. This is so today, and it has always been so.

Never once did Bildad appeal to divine revelation. His authority was the fathers, not God. Men will not be judged at the Great White Throne of God by tradition or on the basis of assumption or simply by appearance, the way it looks on the surface. They will be judged on the facts as God knows them to be.

We certainly judge men by what they do or by what we think they do. Yet our own personal biases may enter into the way we judge the actions of others.

Our Lord said to the Scribes and Pharisees: "If any man hear my words, and believe not, I judge him not: for I came not to judge the world, but to save the world. He that rejecteth me, and receiveth not my words, hath one that judgeth him: the word that I have spoken, the same shall judge him in the last day" (John 12:47,48). We will all be judged by the standards of God and not the standards of men. Men judge by appearance or by tradition based on the wisdom of the fathers, either past or present; but God is the final Judge.

Bildad said that God would not allow unfortunate things to come to the righteous but would fill them with gladness and laughter. "Behold," said Bildad, "as surely as God will never uphold wrongdoers, He will never cast away a blameless man. He will yet fill your mouth with laughter, Job, and your lips with joyful shouting. Those who hate you will be clothed with shame, and the tent of the wicked shall be no more" (Job 8:20-22). This was how Bildad argued but he had no foundation for it. To suggest that afflictions are only for the wicked and that a good man will not experience them is not true to the methods of God. This is part of the false wisdom of the ancients.

Zophar

Zophar was the third friend to visit Job and most likely the youngest of the three. According to the standards of those days, being younger than the others, he is not considered to be as wise as they. Only two of his speeches are recorded, one in chapter 11 and the other in chapter 20.

Again we will just summarize what he has to say and examine his particular approach to the problem.

Zophar is the most dogmatic of the three. He assumes many things and then states his conclusion with a finality that brooks no opposition. For Job to differ with Zophar's conclusions is proof, in Zophar's eyes, that Job is a sinner.

There are people like that today. They are so sure of what they say that anyone who disagrees with them calls forth their scorn or anger.

Here are some of his dogmatisms. He said to Job in chapter 11:6: "Know therefore that God exacts of you less than your guilt and iniquity deserve." This was typical of this man's approach. He knew what all this was about. He knew that though Job suffered great reverses and great hardships, he actually deserved to suffer even more.

He even accused Job of lying and of mocking God. He said, "Should your boastings and babble make men keep silent? And when you mock and scoff, shall no man make you ashamed?" (v. 3).

Then Zophar called on Job for repentance. He said, "If you set your heart aright and stretch out your hands to God; If you put sin out of your hand and far away from you, and let not evil dwell in your tent; Then can you lift up your face to Him without stain of sin and unashamed; yea, you shall be steadfast and secure; you shall not fear" (vv. 13-15).

Zophar was a legalist and formalist. He had no right sense of God's character at all. He had a certain amount of truth but it was distorted because it was not complete.

There are those who argue today that God is a God of love. This is true, but from this they try to do away with hell saying that God will never punish a person in hell for all eternity. They fail to realize that the same Book that shows God is a God of love also declares Him to be a God of justice. God will not overlook sin. He has provided for the sinner through the sacrifice of Christ; but if the sinner rejects the great price paid for him, then there is nothing left but eternal separation from God.

Though God warns of judgment He first offers salvation through grace. God is not against men, He is for them. He does not exact from us according to the letter of the law but is instead a liberal giver. This is what the

Scriptures show again and again. Look at Romans 5:8 for a good example: "God commendeth his love toward us, in that, while we were yet sinners, Christ died for us." God will exact punishment for sin, but He has provided a substitute for the sinner if the sinner will accept that substitute.

When men like Zophar assume what is untrue and call for repentance on the basis of their false assumptions, they only stir up anger. God, of course, allowed these men to use their arguments against Job. The Lord wanted to help him see that though he had not been guilty of specific sins that would have brought calamities upon him, nevertheless he needed his character to be refined under God's hand. Job needed to be broken, for he was proud. But we cannot force men into seeing this by sheer dogmatism on our part. We do not bring a man to repentance by clubbing him.

A tendency in human nature is that when one person tries to force his opinions on another, the one will refuse to listen to anything the other has to say.

God brought Job to the place of repentance but He used a different method than any of these so-called comforters. They needed the truth given in Romans 2:3,4: "And thinkest thou this, O man, that judgest them which do such things, and doest the same, that thou shalt escape the judgment of God? Or despisest thou the riches of his goodness and forbearance and longsuffering; not knowing that the goodness of God leadeth thee to repentance?" This is God's approach. This is His method.

CHAPTER SEVEN

JOB ANSWERS HIS
SO-CALLED FRIENDS

None of these so-called friends understood Job nor did they know God's character or His ways in dealing with His child. On the other hand, Job was not the kind of man to sit quietly by and allow men whom he knew personally to say what they did without defending himself. They did not bring him to self-judgment. They only stirred up the spirit of self-vindication in him. They said good things and true things but not the whole truth. They argued from experience and tradition and legalism, but Job was not convinced by their arguments. Neither was he silent.

It is no wonder that he satirized them with words, declaring that they thought they were the people and that wisdom would die with them. Then he went on to say that he had understanding as well as they and he was not a whit inferior to them. He called them forgers of lies and physicians of no value. He wanted them to hold their peace. Their silence would be wisdom. He called them miserable comforters. So far as arguments are concerned, Job had the better of them; but this did not solve his problem.

Job's friends with their counsels did not lead him to self-judgment but ministered rather to his spirit of self-vindication. They spoke of God but not in a way that really introduced Him into the scene. They said some true things but they did not speak all truth. They called on experience and tradition and legality for what these could furnish by way of authority and insight, but they missed the core of the matter. It is no wonder that Job, humanly speaking, reacted as he did and heaped scorn upon their heads. He told them that their silence would have been more beneficial than their advice. They were miserable comforters indeed!

So far as argument is concerned, it would seem that Job had the better of it but someone in a situation such as Job's does not need argument—he needs the truth of the Word of God. Job gave way at times to some passionate and pointed utterances which he later regretted.

But how would we react to the suffering Job was passing through and at the same time have so much slander heaped upon us?

God has tested me sometimes in such situations, and I have found there is a good deal of the old self that wants to fight back.

Job's friends argued that God only punishes the wicked and gives prosperity to the upright. This is saying that only the wicked suffer. But this is not scriptural. One of them said that the wicked always suffer. And still another said that prosperity of the wicked is short-lived. But this is not the true picture of real life.

Job pointed out from his observations that both the righteous and the wicked suffer. Yet not all the wicked suffer, for some of them seem to have an easy time of it all through life. And the prosperity of the wicked is not always short-lived. Sometimes it passes from one generation to the next and several generations after that.

None of Job's friends understood God or the ways of God. But Job himself, though he had a better understanding of how life was among men, also missed some things.

So the discussions ended in a deadlock. No one got anywhere.

Job, after scorning his friends, cried out for pity. There is a place for sympathy, and there are times when we all need it. Apparently these friends had little or none to give Job, and in this they again were wrong. However, their being wrong did not make Job right. He was anything but a meek man at this juncture in these discussions. He had not reached the end of himself. Yet this was what God was after. We know this because God has let us see behind the scenes. There was no specific sin in Job's life that warranted calamities such as had befallen him. But Job was not without faults and God permitted these troubles to come to him in order to refine his spiritual life.

Job was full of self-vindication and of anger against his friends. He had some mistaken thoughts about God, too. And at the time his friends gave up their discussion with Job, they were far from being reconciled to him.

A Wrong Approach

He himself was unbroken and unsubdued in heart. Their treatment was wrong, of course, and so they hurt rather than helped. Nevertheless, if Job had humbled himself and had admitted that he in himself was nothing, he would have been closer to reaching a solution to this whole matter. At the same time he was not guilty of committing gross sins which brought on these calamities.

This was why their admonition for him to repent did not make sense.

Had they spoken softly and tenderly to Job, they would have been more likely to have melted him down. As it was, their attitude begot a like attitude in him. So, by the time Zophar was through with his final discourse, Job and his visitors were at a standoff.

Job could see nothing wrong with himself, and his friends could see nothing right with him. With all of their wrangling and accusing of each other they got nowhere. It is easy to get led into a trap of this nature. The only way out of it is to look away unto Jesus the Author and Finisher of our faith, who for the joy that was set before Him endured the cross, despising the shame and is set down at the right hand of the throne of God. A good many of our problems would be solved if we would make Christ the center of our living and being.

Job was determined to maintain his integrity. His friends were determined to pick holes in him and find faults and flaws of all kinds. There was no common ground of understanding between them. We will see how God remedied this situation by bringing another person into the picture, but this must be left for a later discussion.

Life's Two Sides

Job saw the brevity of life and its miseries. He emphasized, however, only the dark side of things. This is the way many others are doing. This is the easiest side of life to see. The Devil will make sure, as we let him, that we see only the depressing and sad side of things. It is only when we are in true contact and relationship with God that life takes on another color entirely. This is what the Psalmist did and he found that God "hath not dealt with us after our sins; nor rewarded us according to our iniquities. For as the heaven is high above the earth, so great is his mercy toward them that fear him" (Ps. 103: 10,11).

When I begin to think that God has dealt with me too hard, I read this Psalm and then admit that He hasn't really dealt with me at all according to my sins or rewarded me according to my iniquities. The Lord has removed our guilt and transgressions as far from us as the east is from the west. And as a father pitieth his children so the Lord pities those who fear Him. God knows our frame and remembers that we are dust.

It is well to remember that man's days are as grass. "As a flower of the field, so he flourisheth. For the wind passeth over it, and is gone; and the place thereof shall know it no more. But the mercy of the Lord is from everlasting to everlasting upon them that fear him, and his righteousness unto children's children" (Ps. 103:15-17).

Job's Strange Reactions

Job did not see the mercy of God. He spoke rather of the wrath of God and the difficulties that man had to face. Here are his words: "Is there not an appointed warfare and time of probation to man upon earth? And are not his days like the days of a hireling? As a servant earnestly longs for the shade and evening shadows, and as a hireling who looks for the reward of his work, So am I allotted months of futile suffering, and [long] nights of misery are appointed to me. When I lie down, I say, When shall I arise, and the night be gone? And I am full of tossings to and fro till the dawning of the day. My flesh is clothed with worms and clods of dust; my skin is broken and become loathsome, and it closes up and breaks out afresh. My days are swifter than a weaver's shuttle, and are spent without hope. Oh, remember that my life is but wind—a puff, a breath, a sob; my eye shall see good no more" (Job 7:1-7).

Job seems to think of God as his enemy who has intentions of evil against him. Beginning with verse 11 of the same chapter he says: "Therefore I will not restrain my mouth; I will speak in the anguish of my spirit; I will complain in the bitterness of my soul, O Lord! Am I a sea, or a sea monster that You set a watch over me? When I say, My bed shall comfort me, my couch shall ease my complaint, Then You scare me with dreams, and terrify me through visions; So that I would choose strangling and death rather than these my bones. I loathe my life; I would not live for ever. Let me alone, for my days are a breath—falsity, futility" (7:11-16).

As we have pointed out so many times before, Job did not see all that was going on behind the scenes. He did not realize what God was actually doing in his life, but we can see these things and should profit from them. What are our attitudes when difficult situations confront us? Do we get all stirred up inside against God, asking why He has done this to us? Sometimes people have become so bitter that they have actually renounced God.

Perhaps God allows a loved one to be called home after an illness, brief or long, and someone says, "If that's what God does, I don't want anything to do with Him."

That is the response of a petulant child, not of a trusting and mature believer. What God allows to come into our lives, He allows for a good purpose.

In the last part of the 7th chapter Job speaks about his sin but there seems to be no real conviction about it. He is more interested in getting rid of his afflictions than he is of finding out what God is seeking to do. Here are Job's words: "If I have sinned, what harm have I done You, or what can I do about it, O You watcher and keeper of men? Why have You set me as a mark for You, so that I am a burden to myself and You? And why do You not pardon my transgression and take away my iniquity? For now shall I lie down in the dust, and [even if] You will seek me diligently, [it will be too late, for] I shall not be" (7:20,21).

These are strange words to come from a man like Job. But let us remember that in the anguish of his soul and in the pain of his body he is saying things that at another time he regrets. Death to him seems to be the only way out. He admits that he is a sinner but he wonders why God punishes him instead of showing mercy. Actually this is not punishment but discipline that God is permitting. At this point Job does not know the difference.

The patriarch's first reply is full of bitterness against God and against man. He has not learned, in New Testament language, what it is to be controlled by the Spirit of Christ. Job did not have the revelation of God and Christ that we have; consequently, we would sin against greater light if we spoke against God as he did. Yet deep down in our hearts we know that we have sometimes reacted toward God in this very same manner.

The one example of perfection, of course, is our Saviour Himself. He suffered as no man ever suffered, but He never questioned God's character. We read in Hebrews 2:9,10: "But we see Jesus, who is made a little lower than the angels for the suffering of death, crowned with glory and honour; that he by the grace of God should taste death for every man. For it became him, for whom are all things, and by whom are all things, in bringing many sons unto glory, to make the captain of their salvation perfect through sufferings."

In still another passage in Hebrews we learn of another way in which Christ suffered: "Who in the days of his flesh, when he had offered up prayers and supplications with strong crying and tears unto him that was able to save him from death, and was heard in that he feared; Though he were a Son, yet learned he obedience by the things which he suffered." Since this was true of the Son of God, how much more is it true of us! And the same passage goes on to say, "And being made perfect, he became the author of eternal salvation unto all them that obey him" (Heb. 5:7-9).

Job Doubted God's Goodness

Job however doubted God's goodness. And when one begins to doubt God's goodness, that one is in trouble. He said some things about God that later on he abhorred himself for. He repented in dust and ashes; nevertheless he said them.

In chapters 9 and 10 we find Job's answer to Bildad's speech. Though the sufferer may have been speaking quietly there is an undertone of intense bitterness in what he says.

Job begins by saying, "Yes, I know it is true; but how can mortal man be right before God?" (9:2). Job's question on how a man might be just with God has often been used as an evangelistic text. This is quite correct, for we do have the answer; but Job was saying here that he had no answer. Job was sure that if he could find the answer he would not be suffering as he was.

He goes on to say, "If one should want to contend with Him, he cannot answer one [of His questions] in a thousand" (9:3). God's wisdom far surpasses our wisdom. This is good for us to know in our age that pretends to know so much. Had Job followed through his statement logically, he would have been willing to leave the answers to God with regard to his own perplexities.

In 9:4 Job says, "God is wise in heart and mighty in strength; who has ever hardened himself against Him, and prospered or even been safe?" Here Job recognizes that God is supreme and that there is no appeal from whatever God does or decides. He has both wisdom and power so that He can overwhelm any vain attempt to reason with Him. But how terrible it is for a man to say such things as though God were taking advantage of Job. Why did God allow such things to be put in the Book? So that we might take a good look at our own hearts and see if we are any better than Job in this.

It is clear from these words that Job is not a lowly man seeking the true answer to his problems. He is not like Jeremiah who said in a similar situation: "Uncompromisingly righteous and rigidly just are You, O Lord, when I complain and contend with You; yet let me plead and reason the case with You. Why does the way of the wicked prosper? Why are all they at ease and thriving who deal very treacherously and deceitfully? You have planted them, yes, they have taken root; they grow, yes, they bring forth fruit. You are near in their mouth and far from their heart. But You, O Lord, know and understand me and my devotion to You; You have seen me and tried my heart toward You. O Lord, pull these rebellious ones out like sheep for the slaughter, and devote and prepare them for the day of slaughter. How long must the land mourn, and the grass and herbs of the whole country wither? Through the wickedness of those who dwell in it, the beasts and the birds are consumed and are swept away [by the drought], because men mocked me saying, He shall not live to see our final end" (Jer. 12:1-4, Amp.).

Job's Continuing Perplexities

This is not a verse-by-verse study of the Book of Job. We have merely summarized the discourses of Job's friends, and we are doing the same with Job's answers. There are eight of them and they contain some remarkable truths on several subjects. But as we have seen, Job eulogizes God in chapter 9 and yet speaks of God as though He followed the principle that "might is right."

Job's perplexity with God's purposes shows up again in 9:11-15: "Lo, He goes by me, and I see Him not; He passes on also, but I perceive Him not. Behold, He snatches away; who can hinder or turn Him back? Who will say to Him, What are You doing? God will not withdraw His anger; the proud helpers of Rahab [proud and arrogant monster of the sea] bow under Him. How much less shall I answer Him, choosing out my words to reason with Him? Whom, though I were righteous—upright and innocent— yet I could not answer; I must appeal for mercy to my opponent and judge—for my right." Job concludes that the only way he can come to God is to appeal for mercy. But even then he believes that since he is innocent there is no point in appealing for mercy.

He continues this train of thought in verse 16: "If I called, and He answered me, yet would I not believe that He listened to my voice. For He overwhelms and breaks me with a tempest, and multiplies my wounds without cause. He will not allow me to catch my breath, but fills me with bitterness" (9:16-18). In all of this Job is still claiming complete innocence, not realizing, as we shall see later, that though he has not been guilty of specific gross sins, there is nevertheless a need of refining in his life.

Job goes on to say that if it is a contest of strength between him and God then, of course, God is almighty. If it is a matter of justice, who has the right to summon God or argue with Him?

He continues his lament: "Though I am innocent and in the right, my own mouth would condemn me; though I am blameless, He would prove me perverse. Though I am blameless, I regard not myself; I despise my life— though I am innocent, let God destroy me! It is all one; therefore I say, God [does not discriminate, but] destroys the blameless and the wicked" (9:20-22). Job will later abhor himself for saying such things and repent in dust and ashes.

Job Longs for a Mediator

The patriarch is conscious that he needs help. He longs for the "daysman" to stand between him and God. Another translation of this word "daysman" is "umpire." Perhaps we would understand it better as "redeemer." This is brought before us in the following section: "I shall be held guilty and be condemned; why then should I labor in vain [to appear innocent]? If I wash myself with snow, and cleanse my hands with lye, Yet You will plunge me into the ditch, and my own clothes will abhor me and refuse to cover [so foul a body]. For God is not a mere man, as I am, that I should answer Him, that we should come together in court. There is no umpire between us, who might lay his hand upon us both—would that there were!" (9:29-33).

The King James Version reads: "Neither is there any daysman betwixt us, that might lay his hand upon us both. Let him take his rod away from me, and let not his fear terrify me: Then would I speak, and not fear him; but it is not so with me" (9:33-35).

Job's argument is that he is not wicked in the sense his friends have said he is; but he feels the need of someone to mediate between himself and God. Yet he believes that if he is already pronounced wicked by God whom he has just described, then it is in vain that he protests his innocence. This is why he needs someone to come between him and God, someone to represent him and his cause. A little later Job comes to know there is a Daysman, an Umpire, a Redeemer, a Mediator between him and God.

Do we know and appropriate this truth? Christ is the Mediator between God and man. There is no other. He has died for our sins and He alone can speak for us before the Father. Have we placed our case in His hands? Those who are unsaved must receive Him as personal Saviour. Those who are saved look to Him to keep their relationship between them and God intact.

Perhaps you as a believer have been passing through hard trials and you feel the need of someone to help you. This same Mediator of whom we speak has suffered in all points as we have, but He has passed through His testings without sin. He understands us and all about us, and will plead our case.

God is not the kind of God that Job describes Him to be in this section of the book. There is mercy with God and not injustice. We deserve judgment for sin, but our Mediator will plead our case in mercy.

Job did not lose faith in the fact that God is, but he lost sight of the fact of God's goodness. From the depths of his suffering Job cried: "I will say to God, Do not condemn me—do not make me guilty! Show me why You contend with me. Does it seem good to You that You should oppress, that You should despise and reject the work of Your hands, and favor the schemes of the wicked? Have You eyes of flesh? Do You see as man sees? Are Your days as the days of man, are Your years as man's years, That You inquire after my iniquity and search for my sin, Although You know that I am not wicked or guilty and there is none who can deliver me out of Your hand?

"Your hands have formed me and made me, and would You turn round and destroy me? Remember (earnestly), I beseech You, that You have fashioned me as clay [out of the same earth-material, exquisitely and elaborately], and will You bring me into dust again? Have You not poured me out as milk and curdled me like cheese? You have clothed me with skin and flesh, and have knit me together with bones and sinews. You have granted me life and favor, and Your providence has preserved my spirit. Yet the present evils have You hid in Your heart [for me since my creation]; I know that this was in Your purpose and thought. If I sin, then You observe me, and You will not acquit me from my iniquity and guilt. If I were wicked, woe unto me! And if I am righteous, yet must I not lift up my head, for I am filled with disgrace and the sight of my affliction. If I lift myself up, You hunt me like a lion, and again show Yourself inflicting marvelous trials upon me" (10:2-16).

This is not a true view of God. God does not despise the works of His hands. He does not favor the wicked over the righteous. He did not create man in order to treat him as Job thought he was being treated. Job thought God was picking on him, but this was far from the truth.

God has allowed Satan to test this servant who was possibly the most outstanding believer of his day. He was a good man but he was a man who had a sinful nature as all of us have. There are things deep down inside all of us that we little suspect until circumstances are such as to draw them out. This is what happened to Job; but all he saw at this particular time was his trials, and dark despair settled upon him. He was weary of life and for this reason poured out his thoughts to God, many of which were against God.

CHAPTER EIGHT

JOB ANSWERS HIS
SO-CALLED FRIENDS (continued)

Job's Forthrightness

We cannot help but note the forthrightness of this man who plainly says to God that he doubts the wisdom of what God was doing with him. At a later time Job will rise to remarkable spiritual heights. He came to the place where he said, "Though he slay me, yet will I trust in him: but I will maintain mine own ways before him. He also shall be my salvation: for an hypocrite shall not come before him." Job goes from depths of despair to heights of faith, something that all of us who know a little about our own hearts' responses in times of trial will recognize and appreciate. His view of God is his stumbling block here. He recognizes that God is almighty and can do with His servants as He pleases. But instead of seeing God as a God of love and justice and mercy, Job looks upon God's actions as arbitrary. God who knows the end from the beginning is never arbitrary.

Job's friends kept pointing to him as being both a hypocrite and a liar. They mockingly suggested that he should seek out God because God was exacting less from him than he deserved. Yet Job, in spite of the cloud over his heart and mind, will not allow God to be belittled. Here are some of the things he said in chapter 12: "No doubt you are the only wise people [in the world], and wisdom will die with you!" (v.2). Then beginning with verse 9 through 25 he says, "Who is so blind as not to recognize in all these [that good and evil are promiscuously

scattered throughout nature and human life] that it is
God's hand which does it and God's way? In His hand
is the life of every living thing and the breath of all mankind. Is it not the task of the ear to discriminate between
wise and unwise words, just as the mouth distinguishes
beween desirable and undesirable food? With the aged
[you say] is wisdom; and with length of days comes understanding. But only with God is [perfect] wisdom and
might; He alone has [true] counsel and understanding.

"Behold, He tears down, and it cannot be built again;
He shuts a man in, and none can open. He withholds the
waters, and the land dries up; again, He sends forth rains,
and they overwhelm the land or transform it.

"With Him are might and wisdom; the deceived and
the deceiver are His and in His power. He leads [great
and scheming] counselors away stripped and barefoot, and
makes the judges fools [in human estimation, by over-
throwing their plans]. He looses the fetters ordered by
kings, and has the waistcloth [of a slave] bound about their
own loins. He leads away priests as spoil, and men firmly
seated He overturns. He deprives of speech those who are
trusted, and takes away the discernment and discretion
of the aged. He pours contempt on princes, and loosens
the belt of the strong—disabling them, bringing low the
pride of the learned. He uncovers deep things out of darkness, and brings out to light black gloom and the shadow
of death.

"He makes nations great, and He destroys them; He
enlarges nations and then straitens and shrinks them
again, and leads them away captive. He takes away understanding from the leaders of the people of the land and
of the earth, and causes them to wander in a wilderness
where there is no way. They grope in the dark without
light, and He makes them to stagger and wander like a
drunken man."

God to Job was a great God, even though Job contended with Him. And knowing man as well as he did,

Job would not take his case to any man but would carry it into the presence of God. Then in his despair he cried out: "O, if I could only find Him." Have we not all passed through these periods in life when we felt that the heavens were brass? Yet such is not the truth. All the time we were groaning under our perplexities and afflictions God was working for our good and His glory.

Job did not have the Bible to read and study to find the answers to his problems. As far as we know, the Book of Job was the first portion of God's Word that was put in writing. Job had to go on the basis of what revelation was accorded him at that time; but we have the Bible from Genesis to Revelation and know of Christ who is the Mediator between God and men.

Job Wants to Plead His Own Case

In chapter 13 Job again speaks quite forcibly of his refusal to let his friends arbitrate his case for him. He declares he will take it to God himself. Job quite brusquely brushes his friends aside and tells them that what they know he knows, that he is not a bit inferior to them. He follows this with the following discourse.

"Surely I wish to speak to the Almighty, and I desire to argue and reason my case with God [that He may explain the conflict between what I believe of Him and what I see of Him]. But you are forgers of lies—you defame my character most untruthfully; you are all physicians of no value and have no remedy to offer. Oh, that you would altogether hold your peace! Then you would evidence your wisdom, and might pass for wise men.

"Hear now my reasoning, and listen to the pleading of my lips. Will you speak unrighteously for God, and talk deceitfully for Him? Will you show partiality to Him—be unjust to me in order to gain favor with Him? Will you act as special pleaders for God? Would it be profitable for you if He should investigate your tactics [with me]? Or as one deceives and mocks a man, do you deceive and mock Him? He will surely reprove you, if you do secretly show partiality. Shall not His majesty make you afraid, and should not your awe for Him restrain you? Your memorable sayings are proverbs of ashes— valueless; your defenses are defenses of clay [and will crumble]. Hold your peace! Let me alone, so I may speak, and let come on me what will.

"Why should I take my flesh in my teeth, and put my life in my hand [incurring the danger of God's wrath]? [I do it because] though He slay me, yet will I wait for and trust Him—and behold, He will slay me; I have no hope; nevertheless I will maintain and argue my ways before Him—even to His face. This will be my salvation, that a polluted and godless man shall not come before Him. Listen diligently to my speech, and let my declaration be in your ears. Behold now, I have prepared my case; I know that I shall be justified and vindicated" (13:3-18).

It goes without saying that Job's words to his friends and some of their words to him are hardly patterns for believers to use. There is a great deal of bitterness on both sides.

Job was suffering greatly in body and mind and the discourses of his friends had added torment to his already overburdened heart. To use some of our modern expressions, he "exploded" in his resentment against their unfair treatment. At times he "blew off steam," and yet intermingled with his strong words were often statements of remarkable truth concerning God. From what we have already seen in chapter 13 Job stated that even if God slew him, yet he would wait and trust Him.

Then beginning with verse 18 Job pleads his case. He said, "Behold now, I have prepared my case; I know that I shall be justified and vindicated. Who is he who will argue against and refute me? For then I would hold my peace and expire" (13:18,19). Job went on to plead with

God to make known to Him what his transgressions were. Why should God hide His face from His servant and alienate him as if he were an enemy?

If a Man Die?

The 14th chapter begins with these words: "Man that is born of a woman is of few days and full of trouble. He comes forth like a flower, and withers; he flees also like a shadow, and continues not. And [Lord] do You open Your eyes upon such a one, and bring me into judgment with you?" (vv. 1-3). Job expresses thoughts on death, its inevitability and mysteries. Then he raises a question that touches all of us: "If a man die, shall he live again?" (v. 14).

Apparently Job answered, at least in part, his own question in 19:25-27. He declared, "For I know that my Redeemer and Vindicator lives, and at last—the Last One —He will stand upon the earth; And after my skin, even this body, has been destroyed, then from my flesh or without it I shall see God, Whom I, even I, shall see for myself and on my side! And my eyes shall behold Him, and not as a stranger! My heart pines away and is consumed within me."

Job knew that one day the Lord would vindicate him. He could not trust these earthly friends but he did trust God. God as his Vindicator would appear on earth, and Job knew that he himself would see God. Not only that, but he would see God on his side. His Redeemer would be his Vindicator. Though Job may have had no hope for the time when he was suffering, he looked forward to the great resurrection day when God would vindicate him. He looked forward to the time when his Living Redeemer would change that poor, weak and decaying body of Job's into a glorified body. Then he would see God face to face and learn the secret of all his sorrow.

Job did not have the New Testament revelation that we have. Yet he had foregleams of great truths concerning God's great end-time program. He believed God and trusted Him for it. So in spite of all his difficulties, Job still showed himself to be a man of faith. Such a man would not be defeated in the end but would find the victory through faith.

Job's constant cry was that he might find God. God was not really far away. He was very near to His servant, but Job, because of his heart condition before God, was not aware of this great fact. In chapter 23 the patriarch cried out again against the troubles that had befallen him and his desire to find God: "Oh, that I knew where I might find Him, that I might come even to His seat! I would lay my cause before Him, and fill my mouth with arguments. I would learn what He would answer me, and understand what He would say to me. Would He plead against me with His great power? No; He would give heed to me. There the righteous—one who is upright and in right standing with God—could reason with Him; so I should be acquitted by my Judge for ever. Behold, I go forward and to the east, but He is not there; or backward and to the west, but I cannot perceive Him; On the left hand and to the north, where He works [I seek Him], but I cannot behold Him; He turns Himself to the right hand and the south, but I cannot see Him" (23:3-9).

After having said all these things, Job made the following remarkable statement concerning God. Here again Job's faith came to the surface and he rose above his circumstances: "But He knows the way that I take—He has concern for it, appreciates and pays attention to it. When He has tried me, I shall come forth as refined gold [pure and luminous]" (23:10).

Job and Other Troubled Persons

Can we say this when we pass through trials? In spite of all the added light we have is this our conclusion? Job's experience is a living experience for us to learn from. In spite of his anguish of spirit and his bitter words Job had not turned against God. He lost sight of Him temporarily, but he did not renounce Him. A check through the Scriptures will reveal that Job was not the only one who passed through such spiritual situations.

The Psalmist said in Psalm 102:1,2: "Hear my prayer, O Lord, and let my cry come unto thee. Hide not thy face from me in the day when I am in trouble; incline thine ear unto me: in the day when I call answer me speedily." Perhaps these words describe our experiences. We are in the midst of trouble and want a speedy answer from God. The Psalmist felt even as Job did and as we do: "Why standest thou afar off, O Lord? why hidest thou thyself in the time of trouble?" (Ps. 10:1).

The same thought is given in Psalm 88:14: "Lord, why castest thou off my soul? why hidest thou thy face from me?"

But even more than that, David spoke prophetically of our Lord Jesus Christ when he said in Psalm 22, "My God, my God, why hast thou forsaken me? Why art thou so far from helping me, and from the words of my roaring? O my God, I cry in the daytime, but thou hearest not; and in the night season, and am not silent" (vv. 1,2). Yet there was no bitterness in our Lord's cry. He ascribes holiness to God and vindicated the character of God in the midst of the sufferings on Calvary: "But thou art holy, O thou that inhabitest the praises of Israel" (v. 3).

Reading in the daily devotional booklet, *Daily Bread*, I noticed this particular statement from John Hall: "I stood one evening watching the pure white flower on a vine encircling my veranda. I had been told that the bud which hung with closed petals all day unfolded every evening and in the dark of night sent out the most lovely fragrance. It was true. The miracle was more than I had anticipated. A feeling of awe possessed me as I saw bud after bud, as under the touch of an invisible hand, slowly emerging into full bloom and beauty. I felt that if the finger of God laid upon these flowers could do this in a way beyond the power of man to explain, can we doubt the divine touch in an hour of darkness that will also make us bloom forth and send out the fragrance of His grace? God's choicest plans are developed in the shade."

The following letter is one that the writer gave me permission to use. Of course, the author's name will not be given. This person wrote in part: "This letter is most difficult for me, yet I must have some assurance of life or life is nothing. I do earnestly pray that what you said about no one being too far from God is true. I have poured out my heart before God, and my blood runs cold and fear grips my heart when I think of what I have done. I feel like God has cut me off. But, oh, if there is still a chance for me, I would be eternally grateful.

"There came seasons of coldness in my life. I did not read the Word of God nor did I pray, so I became an easy prey for Satan. If I had kept faithful to Jesus, none of the following would have happened. I had warnings from God as to my actions. He reminded me that my body was the temple of the Holy Spirit. I felt somehow that I could make it right with God, and I used David's sin for an excuse.

"I cannot describe the fear and conviction that grips my soul today. I tell you that I have tasted hell. I have this horror of being cut off from God. The thing is that I know I am saved . . . I have begged God for forgiveness and I have confessed day and night these horrible things to Him. Since I have been in the Word, I have been completely overwhelmed. I have seen the horrors of what I have done. I feel my heart would fail me for fear.

"I know that one day I shall stand before Him. This cannot be avoided. I know that Jesus can save and only His blood can cleanse. I have forsaken my sins. I have given myself to the Lord and have asked Him to take me back.

"If only I could blot out this year. I want only God and His will. I have begged and begged Him to forgive me. I know God has mercy and I want that mercy for myself. I have learned a great lesson and I will never willingly or knowingly depart from Him again. I need your help badly. After all I have done, will God forgive all these sins that have wrought such scars, and will God take me back? He knows I am desperate without Him.

"On your broadcast you said we are never too far from God. I hope and pray that this is really true. I have sinned against light and what a horrible thing that is. Yet I cling to Him for help."

I answered her letter, pointing out that her present problem was her lack of faith in God's promises. First John 1:9 says that if we confess our sins, God is faithful and just to forgive us our sins and to cleanse us from all unrighteousness. So I urged her to accept this as God's assurance to her. He wanted to forgive her, but she had been refusing to accept His forgiveness.

She wrote back a letter of joy and victory. God's peace was controlling her heart because she had taken Him at His Word.

Comforting Passages

There is forgiveness for such. First John 1:9 is a clear answer to this. Psalm 51 also shows that God is merciful. Psalm 139 is equally clear in this respect. Job did not have these passages of Scripture to comfort him but we have. They tell us how men and women who had departed from God were restored to fellowship once more.

David wrote: "O Lord, thou hast searched me, and known me. Thou knowest my downsitting and mine uprising, thou understandest my thought afar off. Thou compassest my path and my lying down, and art acquainted with all my ways. For there is not a word in my tongue, but, lo, O Lord, thou knowest it altogether. Thou hast beset me

behind and before, and laid thine hand upon me. Such
knowledge is too wonderful for me; it is high, I cannot
attain unto it.

"Whither shall I go from thy spirit? or whither shall
I flee from thy presence? If I ascend up into heaven, thou
art there: If I make my bed in hell, behold, thou art there.
If I take the wings of the morning, and dwell in the utter-
most parts of the sea; Even there shall thy hand lead me,
and thy right hand shall hold me. If I say, Surely the
darkness shall cover me; even the night shall be light
about me. Yea, the darkness hideth not from thee; but
the night shineth as the day: the darkness and the light
are both alike to thee. For thou hast possessed my reins:
thou hast covered me in my mother's womb. . . . How
precious also are thy thoughts unto me, O God; how great
is the sum of them! If I should count them, they are more
in number than the sand: when I awake, I am still with
thee" (139:1-18).

Let us never be tempted to think that God is far from
us at any time. No matter what the situation is God is
right there. He knows every agony and pain of our hearts.
He understands all about us and our manner of life. If
He seems to temporarily stand aloof, it is only in order
that He might draw us closer to Himself. He wants us to
learn to trust Him, to believe that what He is doing is
for our best. He wants us to trust in the truth of His
Word and not be swayed by the changing feelings of our
hearts.

Job would have much sooner reached the end of his
perplexities and his search for God if he could have admitted that God had not dealt with him after his sins.
In Psalm 103:8 we read: "The Lord is merciful and gracious,
slow to anger, and plenteous in mercy. He will not always
chide: neither will he keep his anger forever. He hath
not dealt with us after our sins; nor rewarded us according
to our iniquities. For as the heaven is high above the

earth, so great is his mercy toward them that fear him. . . .
Like as a father pitieth his children, so the Lord pitieth
them that fear him. For he knoweth our frame; he re-
membereth that we are dust." These are good Psalms for
us to read and reread when we are tempted to look on
life and on God as Job did.

Job's Final Arguments

Job's final rebuttal to his friends is found in chapters
26 through 31. This has been called his final monologue,
for the others are through. They have offered what they
thought was the solution to Job's problems, but he had
out-argued them until they had nothing more to say.

In chapters 26 and 27 Job shows his faith is still in
God. Even though he cannot find a way of communicating
with God, he nevertheless believes that God is.

In the 28th chapter Job shows he has great knowledge
and wisdom and understanding of many mysteries of God's
creation. He concludes the chapter with these words, "And
unto man he said, Behold, the fear of the Lord, that is wisdom; and to depart from evil is understanding" (v. 28, KJV).

It is one thing to have a knowledge of great areas of
truth pertaining to life but it is another thing to know
the basics of spiritual life. Job had not learned the lesson
of humility and of total submission to God. We are reminded in I Corinthians 13 that even though we speak
with tongues of men and of angels and have not love we
are but sounding brass or a tinkling cymbal. This is the
way we are left as we read the 28th chapter of Job and
learn what Job said on that occasion. Job's problem was
that he was justifying himself and not God.

The only way to justify God is to admit that we are
totally depraved, sin-drenched and lost. The more we are
satisfied with self the more hopeless is our situation. Who
are we going to justify when calamities come, if sickness
comes, or heartaches? Are we going to say we do not de-

serve them? or are we going to admit that God has not dealt with us to the degree of our sinfulness? Job was still holding on to his righteousness and would not let it go. He said his heart would not reproach him as long as he lived (27:6).

Job Glories in Past Achievements

In the following three chapters Job brings himself to the forefront. In my course of studying these chapters I took a red pencil and circled the pronouns where Job referred to himself. The picture that resulted reminded me of a child with the chickenpox.

Now we admit that in a biographical sketch the personal pronouns are bound to be used quite often. But here it seems to me to be overdone. It is the proud self that Job emphasizes as he goes back over the days of his splendor and wealth.

He talked about the times when God preserved him and His candle shone over Job's head. Those were the days when Job had plenty and his children were about him. The rock, he said, poured out rivers of oil. "When I went out to the gate of the city, when I prepared my seat in the street—the broad place [for the council at the city's gate]; The young men saw me, and hid themselves; the aged rose up and stood; the princes refrained from talking, and laid their hand on their mouth; The voice of the nobles was hushed, and their tongue cleaved to the roof of their mouth" (vv. 7-10).

When we have to look back into the past to see marks of God's favor, because we can find none in the present, this should be a warning sign. Old age which sees nothing in the future and glories only in the past presents a sad picture indeed. When we are in a situation where the present and the future look dark and we take pride in the past and cannot give God the glory for the present or the future, something is wrong.

Paul had an entirely different outlook on life. He says in Philippians 3 beginning with verse 13: "Brethren, I count not myself to have apprehended: but this one thing I do, forgetting those things which are behind and reaching forth to those things which are before, I press toward the mark for the prize of the high calling of God in Christ Jesus." Even the victories of the past Paul was willing to forget. The matters of yesterday will not do for today. The bright candle of yesterday is but the burnt wick of today. We live in Christ today. Those who look back only to salvation for a testimony have missed out in what the Spirit of God has for them in the present.

No doubt what Job had to say about himself was true. But the Scriptures tell us that we should let another man praise us and not our own mouth. Paul attributed his blessings to the grace of God. Yet some persons will tell us that if we do not blow our own horn, nobody else will do it for us. Paul's answer to all this was: "God forbid that I should glory, save in the cross of our Lord Jesus Christ, by whom the world is crucified unto me, and I unto the world."

Job uses the personal pronouns, "I," "me," "my," some 198 times in chapters 28 through 31. This is how the natural heart finds solace for itself in difficulties. As we look at this, would we do any differently if we were tested as was Job? However, the purpose of God in letting us see this is that we might see ourselves and abhor ourselves as Job eventually abhored himself.

In chapter 29 Job looked at what he had been in the past. In chapter 30 he described his condition after having lost all his possessions and his health. He said, "But now they who are younger than I have me in derision, whose fathers I disdained to set with the dogs of my flock" (v. 1). In verse 9 he said, "And now I have become their song; yes, I am a byword to them. They abhor me, they stand aloof from me, and do not refrain from spitting in my face or at the sight of me. For God has loosed my bow-

string and afflicted and humbled me: they have cast off
the bridle of restraint before me." Up to the time of his
calamities Job was held in esteem; but following them he
was held in disdain. People heaped contempt and derision
upon him. They ˜treated him as an outcast and beneath
them.

Yet as we continue to read on in the Bible we find
that the same things were done to our Lord. In one of
the prophetic Psalms concerning Him we learn: "They that
sit in the gates speak against me; and I was the song of
the drunkards" (69:12). Yet when He was reviled He
reviled not again.

Job did not turn to God in humble contrition. His
pride was cut to the quick by the accusations his friends
made and the treatment he received from those who before had been his inferiors. When pride dwells upon wrongs
done it, bitterness grows.

Turn again to a comparison between Job and our
Lord. In Isaiah 53 we read that Christ "was oppressed,
and he was afflicted, yet he opened not his mouth: he is
brought as a lamb to the slaughter, and as a sheep before
her shearers is dumb, so he openeth not his mouth." Or
as Peter puts it in his First Letter: "Who did no sin,
neither was guile found in his mouth: Who, when he was
reviled, reviled not again; when he suffered, he threatened
not; but committed himself to him that judgeth righteously"
(2:22).

In contrast to Job, you and I who have trusted Christ
have this Christ living in us. So that when we allow Him
to live out His life in us it should be and will be different
than what Job went through. He gave way to a natural
reaction which is the response most of us show, too. When
we remember that Christ lives in us and we allow Him to
fill our beings, our expression of life will be in line with
the kind of life that is in Him. We read in Philippians 2:
"Let this mind be in you, which was also in Christ Jesus:
Who, being in the form of God, thought it not robbery to

be equal with God: But made himself of no reputation, and took upon him the form of a servant, and was made in the likeness of men: And being found in fashion as a man, he humbled himself, and became obedient unto death, even the death of the cross" (vv. 5-8). Humbleness and obedience marked our Lord's life. They will mark ours also when He controls us.

Full trust in the will of God and confidence in the goodness of God make all the difference in how troubles affect us. David wrote at one time, "Why art thou cast down, O my soul? and why art thou disquieted within me? hope thou in God: for I shall yet praise him, who is the health of my countenance, and my God" (Ps. 42:11).

Job Asks to be Weighed in the Balances

In the last chapter of his discourse, chapter 31, Job claimed to be clean. Here is what he said: "I dictated a covenant—an agreement—to my eyes; how then could I look (lustfully) upon a girl?" (v. 1). Not only did Job claim that his actions were pure but his thoughts were pure also. Then he later said, "Does not God see my ways, and count all my steps? If I have walked with falsehood or vanity, or if my foot has hastened to deceit—Oh, let me be weighed in a just balance and let Him weigh me, that God may know my integrity!" (vv. 4-6). Job was willing to be put to the test in this way. He surveyed his own life and character and came to the conclusion that he would welcome an investigation both by God and man. He was sure he would be vindicated. He shows no bitterness at this time. That spirit subsided. But pride is still there.

Job was an unusual man. He had done many noble deeds. He was outstanding in many ways. He was the kind of man who once he became broken before God could be trusted with great things. The Scripture says that the person who is faithful in little things will also be faithful in great things. Pride, however, was still hindering the best that God could do for Job.

So far as knowing the truth of living the Christian life, we are far ahead of Job in the revelation God has given on that subject. We know of the fact of our identification with Christ both in His death and His resurrection. And we know that our "old man is crucified with him." We also know that we are to count this as a fact daily. We do not count our old nature dead but we count ourselves dead to it. And we count ourselves alive to God. When we do this, we do not listen to the desires and suggestions of the old nature but we follow the Lord.

It was no light decision for Job to ask God to weigh him in the balances. Any man apart from Christ would be found wanting. Job was a chaste man, a God-fearing man, kind, and sincere. He was ready to put his signature to the catalog of his own virtues. And he wanted his adversary to put his charges down in writing. Job thought that since he had lived the kind of life he had under the direction of God at other times, everything was all right. He was worthy of the best God could give him. This was his personal evaluation, however. No man is ever worthy of anything from God.

The more we realize our unworthiness the better position we are in for God to use us, provided we yield ourselves to God to do with us and through us what He pleases. Job was a good man who felt himself worthy of the praises of God and men but did not realize that in feeling that way he had put himself outside of the area of usefulness to God. Who can stand before a Thrice Holy God and say that he is clean? Job would say something a little bit later of a different nature.

At the close of the chapter we are told, "The words of Job are ended." Job had called upon earth and man and God and stated his righteousness. But there will be nothing more heard from his lips until he gives honor to whom honor is due. The three friends also had nothing more to say. They ceased to answer Job "because he was righteous in his own eyes."

This last quotation is the key to the problem of Job's own heart. It is also the problem that is at the root of our troubles. Are we righteous in our own eyes when we run into difficulties? Is our first line of defense: "I wonder why this happened to me?" Do we question the goodness and mind of God in such things? The next time Job speaks he speaks a different language.

CHAPTER NINE

ELIHU APPEALS TO JOB

The great principle underlying Job's spiritual problem was given by our Lord. He said, "If any man will come after me, let him deny himself, and take up his cross, and follow me. For whosoever will save his life shall lose it: but whosoever will lose his life for my sake, shall find it." Job's trouble was in trying to save his life, not his physical life but his control over himself and hanging on to the good things he had. If we would have God's best, we must be willing to lay aside everything that might be counted dear to us so that God can really do for us what He wants to do.

When Charles Wesley was first saved, his heart became so full of what the Lord had done for him that he began to write about it in a poem. He wrote stanza after stanza and still had not reached the end. Finally he reached a sort of climax when he wrote:

> "O, for a thousand tongues to sing
> My great Redeemer's praise,
> The glories of my Lord and King,
> The triumphs of His grace."

How different things are when a man is emptied of self.

Job's friends gave up trying to answer him because he was righteous in his own eyes. What can one say to a person who is full of his own importance? In this Job showed a wrong evaluation of himself, and always with this goes a wrong evaluation of God. To have a true evaluation of ourselves we must have a proper evaluation of God. This was what Job lacked.

All the time Job and his friends had been discussing these great matters another person had been sitting listening to all the discourses. His name was Elihu. We learn in Job 32:2 that Elihu's wrath was kindled. This was not a wrath generated by the fallen nature. It was righteous anger because Job had justified himself rather than God.

This anger also embraced Job's three friends because they had not found the answer to Job's problem. They had accused him of many things but they had followed false ideas so had not touched the root of Job's perplexity.

Elihu was the youngest of the four men and he had courteously listened to the discourses of his elders. Now that they were silent, he felt it was permissible for him to speak.

I can almost see him as he listens to the various speeches, getting a bit warm on the inside. "Why don't they get down to the facts? Why don't they speak the truth? Why does Job seek to justify himself? Why doesn't he see himself as God sees him?"

Elihu sized up the matter very clearly. In two brief statements he summarized what was said in the 29 chapters of discourses. He recognized that Job justified himself rather than God. Then he pointed out the problem of the three men. They had condemned Job instead of leading him to condemn himself.

When we justify ourselves we condemn God. But when we condemn ourselves we justify God. We justify God by admitting that He is right in what He is doing, and praising Him for it.

Let God be God

David found solace for his heart in realizing the goodness of God after committing his awful sin. He stated it in these words: "A broken and a contrite heart, O God, thou wilt not despise." Paul says in Romans 3:4: "Let God be true and every man a liar." There is nothing but wrath for the self-righteous. On the other hand, there is nothing but grace for the self-judged. Job was wrong in seeking to defend himself. His friends were wrong in condemning him. The approach of Elihu was something new to this whole problem. He brought God into the picture. He did not argue on the ground of tradition as did Bildad. He did not argue on the ground of legalism as Zophar had. He brought God into the picture. What God says should be an end to all controversy.

With the coming of Elihu we have a new voice, a new approach, a new answer and a new appeal. There was help for Job in what he said and help for us also. What Elihu had to say has become part of the oracles of God for us. The problem surrounding the suffering of the righteous is one that has to be faced by every generation. It is surely not a matter of chance but design that this was the subject of the first book that God gave to men.

Faith Through the Word

In my early experience as a young minister, I sought to increase my personal faith. I read the biographies of some men of God, particularly men who had been noted for their walk of faith. Their experience gave me encouragement and drew me on to learn more concerning this matter. I prayed and waited for months but my faith did not increase. This brought me to the place where I finally cast myself on God in desperation asking, "Why?" Then it was that God gave me a verse I possibly had read before but it had meant little to me. It was Romans 10:17: "So then faith cometh by hearing, and hearing by the word of God." This passage revolutionized my attitude, thinking, preaching, counseling, working—everything. I saw then that if I wanted to increase my faith, I had to go to the Word of God itself. If I wanted to convince others, whether through preaching or writing or counseling, it had to be through the Word. I had to let the Word of God do the job, for faith was the basis of God's working and that faith had to be founded on His Word. We have salvation by faith, sanctification by faith—whatever we need in the spiritual life comes through faith based on His Word.

All through the years since that experience, the predominant thought in my heart and life has been that I must give the Word. People must know: "Thus saith the Lord." Man has no answer for some of the greatest things in life, its deepest mysteries and perplexities. God has and He has given these answers in the Bible.

It was word from God that Elihu brought to Job. It silenced Job and finally, when God was through speaking with him, it brought Job to the place where he went beyond the man that we are introduced to at the beginning of the Book. There he was presented as a good man; but afterwards, by reason of the experiences he had passed through and his response to God, he became a much better man.

The doctrinal aspects of what happened in Job's life are given to us in the New Testament. We are better informed, so far as we know, than was Job concerning these matters, so a greater responsibility lies with us to believe God and appropriate the victory provided for us in Christ. We learn in Romans 6 that through Jesus Christ we have died to the old nature. And we also read in Galatians 2:20 that Christ indwells us. It is this Christ living in us who wants to live out His life through us. This is our privilege by faith. We have been made partakers of the divine nature and have the life of the indwelling Christ to make it possible for us to walk on the victory side of life.

We cannot excuse ourselves by saying, "Well, you know my nature." Yes, we know something about our old natures, but we should also remember that we have new natures. We also have the Holy Spirit indwelling us. He makes Christ real and life-giving in our lives.

We also find in the New Testament that a responsibility lies with those who are spiritual to restore others who have been overtaken in a fault. This is the teaching of Galatians 6:1: "Brethren, if a man be overtaken in a fault, ye which are spiritual, restore such an one in the spirit of meekness; considering thyself, lest thou also be tempted."

Who can say he is spiritual? The moment we boast of our spirituality we give evidence that we do not have it. On the other hand, if we recognize by faith that we have died to sin and that Christ indwells us, that we have the Holy Spirit in us making Christ real to us, then we are spiritual persons. It must be in this frame of mind that we approach the one who has been overtaken in fault. If we deal harshly as did Job's friends and condemn unjustly, we will be of no help. On the other hand, if we come as Elihu did with humility and without pride, knowing that God has the answer for this problem, then we will do good.

Source of Wisdom

Elihu pointed out in Job 32:9 (KJV): "Great men are not always wise: neither do the aged understand judgment." Elihu did not hold to the idea that because a man was old he had more wisdom than one who was younger. This could be true but it is not always true. The greatest wisdom lies with the man who has the Word of God to bring. That Word is sharper than any two-edged sword. It is when the Word of God is presented that the Holy Spirit can take over in a life. Any true wisdom that men have came originally from God. And that wisdom, as James 3:17

says, is from above and "is first pure, then peaceable, gentle, and easy to be intreated, full of mercy and good fruits, without partiality, and without hyprocrisy."

In verse 12 of the same chapter Elihu said, "Yes, I paid attention to what you said, and behold, not one of you convinced Job or made (satisfactory) replies to his words—you could not refute him." Then he went on to warn them: "Beware lest you say, We have found wisdom. God thrusts Job down justly, not man—God alone is dealing with him." The wisdom of these philosophers had missed the mark. They had nothing to boast of.

Then he added: "Now Job has not directed his words against me [therefore I have no cause for irritation], neither will I answer him with speeches like yours. [I speak for truth, not for revenge.]" Job's friends were amazed and embarrassed. They had nothing more to say. Elihu dealt with the subject from an angle they knew little or nothing about. Instead of the wisdom of men with which they were quite familiar, they now were hearing the wisdom of God.

This same response was given to the teaching of our Lord when He preached to the multitudes during His public ministry. "And they were astonished at his doctrine: for he taught them as one that had authority, and not as the scribes" (Mark 1:22).

When Elihu brought in the truth, he also brought in the healing grace of God to the heart. This is always a necessary part in dealing with others. We must not only show men and women where they stand before God because of sin but show also the wonderful grace of God seen in Christ dying for sinners. Job's friends had looked on his ruin and condemned him out of hand. Their method did not convince the sufferer. He merely responded by going to his own defense. We must learn to use the Word of God in grace and in love.

Elihu told the truth about God and then things began

to happen. This prepared the ground for the still small voice of God to speak to Job's heart.

Elihu reminded Job of some of the things he had said: "Surely you have spoken in my hearing, and I have heard the voice of your words, saying, I am clean, without transgression; I am innocent, neither is there iniquity in me; But lo, God finds occasions against me and causes of alienation and indifference; he counts me for His enemy" (33:8-10).

Elihu's answer to this is one we can all ponder to our spiritual benefit: "I reply to you, Behold, in this you are not just; God is superior to man. Why do you contend against Him? For He does not give account of any of His actions. [Sufficient for us it should be to know that it is He Who does them]" (vv. 12,13). What a simple truth this is, yet how little it is understood. If God is greater than man, then obviously God must be the judge of what is right or wrong. This, of course, the proud heart refuses. This is the kind of heart that sits in judgment on God. But who is man to say what is worthy or not worthy of God? Only God Himself can reveal that.

The real secret of all of Job's false reasoning lies right at this point. He did not understand the character of God and the object of God's dealing with him. At a much later time in God's revelation we find these words: "Nay but, O Man, who art thou that repliest against God? Shall the thing formed say to him that formed it, Why hast thou made me thus? Hath not the potter power over the clay, of the same lump to make one vessel unto honour, and another unto dishonour? What if God, willing to shew his wrath, and to make his power known, endured with much longsuffering the vessels of wrath fitted to destruction: And that he might make known the riches of his glory on the vessels of mercy, which he had afore prepared unto glory" (Rom. 9:20-23). This shows that Job's mistake is one common to the human race. It is not for any of us to question the wisdom and character of God or the means He employs to achieve His goals. He is right in both His character and His actions.

God's discipline of His children always has a beneficial purpose. But our benefit from it will depend upon our reaction to it. We may despise it, though according to Hebrews 12, this is something we are not to do. We may faint under it, but here again we are admonished not to. This is possibly what Job had done. A third reaction is that we can be exercised by it and gain from it. Instead of allowing the circumstances to come between us and God, we should keep God between us and the circumstances. This will make all the difference in the world.

Job knew about God but at this particular point, though he recognized the greatness of God, he reacted in self-pity and in despair. What chance did he have in dealing with such a great God? How could a puny man ever get into the presence of God and take up his case before Him?

In contrast to this is David's attitude. He said in Psalm 8:3,4: "When I consider thy heavens, the work of thy fingers, the moon and the stars, which thou has ordained; What is man, that thou art mindful of him? and the son of man, that thou visitest him?" David also saw the greatness of God and he marveled that this great God would consider man and would deal with him as He did.

Job thought man was too insignificant for God to consider. David thanked God that He was so great and so condescending as to deal with man at all.

A Daysman for Job

Job had spoken before of a daysman. He looked for someone to take up his case before God. There is such a Person as we know. There is one Mediator between God and man, the Man Christ Jesus.

In Job's case, Elihu entered into the discussions to serve the place of a daysman. Job had cried: "Oh, for a hearing! Oh, for an answer from the Almighty, and that my adversary would write out His indictment [and put His vague accusations in tangible form] in a book!" (31:35). Elihu came to provide that healing and to get that word from God. There was no need for Job to fear Elihu, for he was formed out of clay as was Job. He was a fellow-mortal though a messenger from God with God's word on his lips. He told Job he would not sit in judgment on him, but rather he would take him by the hand and be a friend to him.

What a beautiful picture this is of Christ. Christ, the eternal Son of God became man in order that He might take our case back to God and represent us before Him. He came from God to bring grace and salvation to us.

In a sense Elihu was going to mediate in this manner also. How much he may have known about Christ, we are not told. Certainly he did not have all the information we have, but he took the approach that reflects the work of Christ on our behalf.

The friends of Job tried to sit as judges against him. Elihu, on the other hand, came to be a brother to him. He sat as Job's equal to plead his case and to present some further truth concerning God. He sat with Job in the fellowship of human sympathy. At the same time he spoke the truth of God to him. This was a new approach in Job's case and was much needed.

The same is needed today. James says, "Who is a wise man and endued with knowledge among you let him show out of a good conversation his works with meekness of wisdom. But if ye have bitter envying and strife in your hearts, glory not, and lie not against the truth. This wisdom descendeth not from above, but is earthly, sensual, devilish. For where envying and strife is, there is confusion and every evil work" (Jas. 3:13-16). The passage does not end here. We have given to us a description of the heavenly wisdom. James said, "But the wisdom that is from above is first pure, then peaceable, gentle, and easy to be intreated, full of mercy and good fruits, without partiality, and without hypocrisy. And the fruit of righteousness is sown in peace of them that make peace" (vv. 17,18).

It was with God's wisdom that Elihu spoke to Job. What a tragedy it would have been had the Book of Job ended at the first verse of chapter 32. Job had ceased speaking and the friends had given up answering him. They were silenced. Had the book ended here there would have been more difficulties raised than had been settled.

On the other hand, if God had broken in on the scene just after Job's friends had ceased, the transition might have been too great for Job. God revealed His majesty and power and with the attitude Job had shown in his discourses, he might have been overwhelmed and filled with fear to where he would not have had an open ear to what God had to say.

So Elihu fits right into the picture bridging the gap between the emptiness of the solutions offered by Job's friends and the final discourse delivered by God Himself.

This was what Ezekiel wrote about in chapter 22 when he recorded God's words: "And I sought for a man among them, which should make up the hedge, and stand in the gap before me for the land, that I should not destroy it: but I found none." Such a person could not be found, so God had no choice but to pour out His indignation upon the land and the people. By their sins they had brought on their own heads the disasters that God sent.

We also read in the New Testament that we who know Christ stand in the gap between God and sinners. Paul wrote in II Corinthians 5:20: "Now then we are ambassadors for Christ, as though God did beseech you by us: we pray you in Christ's stead, be ye reconciled to God."

Elihu felt compulsion to speak. By the time these men were all silenced he could hold his peace no longer. But what he said he wanted to say as a brother. He waited but they offered no further solutions. He could not contain himself. He had to speak. He could not sit quietly by and let things remain deadlocked.

Paul was another who had to preach the gospel. He could not keep quiet. He said that he had nothing to glory in because necessity was laid upon him. "Woe is unto me if I preach not the gospel," he said.

Elihu made it very plain that he was not there to please any man. He was there to give God's message. He said, "I will not [I warn you] be influenced by respect for any man's person and show partiality, neither will I flatter any man. For I know not how to flatter, [wasting my time in mere formalities] for then my Maker would soon take me away [with my divine impulse to utter to you His message]" (32:21,22). We can learn from Elihu to speak God's truth in love without flattering men. Let us learn to speak it in truth and honesty and uprightness and yet with compassion for those with whom we have to deal.

God is Greater Than Man

Elihu's first basic thought in approaching Job and his problem was to make very clear that God is greater than man. This is a fact that must grip our hearts if we are to come up with the right answers in our hours and days of trouble. This is also important if we are dealing with someone who needs help. In using this approach Elihu appealed to Job's conscience and reason. There is a marked absence of abusive and insulting language, quite a contrast to the way Job's friends had spoken to him.

This is in line with Galatians 6:1, a principle we can all lay to heart. We have seen the translation of this verse in the King James Version, but another approach might be helpful: "Even if a man should be detected in some sin my brothers, the spiritual ones among you should quietly set him back on the right path." This is not to be done with a feeling of superiority nor with fanfare. It is to be done quietly with an attitude of heart that guards us against thinking we are immune to such things.

This was the way Elihu sought to help Job. He uncovered Job's faults without stirring up his opposition. This is an art that the Spirit of God imparts if we allow Him to take charge of our counseling with others. Nothing wounds an upright and affectionate man so much as unfounded suspicion and charges growing out of it.

We could well apply that to our situation today among Bible-believing churches and preachers. We need to be careful that we do not let a carnal spirit such as crept into Corinth divide us and hurt us to where the Lord finds it difficult to use us.

Elihu took Job as he found him. He sought to ascertain the facts concerning the patriarch and then spoke in the light of these facts. Elihu did not deal in half truths. He did not assume on the basis of inadequate knowledge as had Job's three friends. He did not entertain suspicion or make unfounded charges. He took Job at his word when he said he was not guilty of specific sin that would have brought these great calamities upon his head.

We are not saying that there was no sin in Job's life. But it did not take the form that Job's friends said it did. Job's problem was inner pride and self-will and the doubting of God's goodness. This is what Elihu brought to Job's attention reminding him of what he had said. He told Job he was not right in this and laid the emphasis upon the fact that God is greater than man. For this reason man has no right or authority to ask God for an explanation of His actions.

God does explain His actions at times to us but He does not need to. The Book of Job itself is an explanation of why God deals as He does in certain lives. But we have no right as human beings to require an explanation from the Sovereign God.

There are bound to be things that God does which are incomprehensible to us. God is infinite and we are finite. He is the Creator and we are the creatures. His ways are higher than our ways and His thoughts than our thoughts. We must let this fact sink deep into our hearts if we are going to have any peace of mind and heart with regard to the everyday happenings of life and God's part in this universe.

CHAPTER TEN

ELIHU APPEALS TO JOB (continued)

God Does Speak

Elihu went on to say that God had spoken not once but many times even though man did not perceive it. And Elihu assured Job that God was still speaking and had something to say to him. What God does, even though it may be incomprehensible to man, is done for the purpose of drawing man back from his own pride of heart and to keep his soul out of the pit. God chastens sometimes by bringing pain and affliction to the human body. But God does this so that His voice may be heard by the one who is ill.

Elihu continued by saying: "[Then third, God's voice may be heard] if there is for the hearer a messenger or an angel, an interpreter, one among a thousand to show to man what is right for him—how to be upright and in right standing with God" (Job 33:23). The help that Job needed was before him in the person of Elihu. He was God's messenger to help the patriarch to come to a right view of himself and of God. A ransom had been paid, the price of redemption had been met. This was the kind of news Job needed. Following this he would come into God's presence with joy and would admit that he had sinned and perverted what was right. He would also acknowledge that God had dealt with him to the full extent of his sin.

An even better explanation of this has been pointed out already in these studies. It is found in Romans 8:28-34. There we learn that all things work together for good to them that love God, to them who are the called according to His purpose. God's purpose is that each person who believes in Christ will be conformed to the image of Christ. Then, since God is for us, who can be against us? Since God spared not His own Son but gave Him up for us all, how shall He not also with Him freely give us all things? Since it is God who justifies, who can lay anything to the charge of His elect? Christ died but is risen again and is seated at the right hand of God. Can anything separate us from that love? No condition or person or power can do so, for that love is in Christ Jesus our Lord.

Elihu assured Job that God was doing the right thing. He also assured the patriarch that his desire was to justify Job before his friends. God was allowing certain things to take place in Job's life to save him from other troubles. Thus Elihu sought to bring Job to a better way of viewing God's Person and acts.

Elihu dealt with facts, not assumptions. He showed Job exactly what he had said. He did not try to misquote him and use wrong charges against him. He presented exactly what Job had said so that Job could defend himself if necessary. But so accurate was Elihu's presentation that Job did not have a word to say.

God Knows What He Is Doing

Elihu's position and basic thought was, God is greater than man. God is God. This means to us that if we are in the midst of trials we should not accuse God of wrongdoing. God knows what He is doing, and what He does for us He does for our good. We should be able to say with Paul that we know all things work together for good. If we are trying to reason trhough our problems let it not be like Job who reasoned from the lesser to the greater and then concluded that he could not find God. Let it rather be like David who reasoned from the greater to the lesser and stand in awe at the condescension of God who would even consider man at all.

Let us seek to find God's standpoint on these things. How could Almighty God, the Perfect One, commit any act of unrighteousness? "Shall not the judge of all the earth do right?" Abraham asked. Paul said it from another angle when he wrote: "Nay but, O man, who art thou that repliest against God?" Our Lord settled it for us when He said, "Even so Father; for it seemed good in thy sight."

If we have been guilty of accusing God, let us turn our eyes upon Jesus, look full in His wonderful face, and the things of earth will grow strangely dim in the light of His glory and grace.

If we follow through the thought back of Elihu's statement that God is greater than man, we will reach entirely different conclusions than Job had reached up to this point. If we could possibly fathom the greatness of God He would be smaller than we are. At least He would be no greater than we are, for if we could understand Him and all about Him He would be someone on our level. But though we have eternity before us, and will know in a future day not as through a glass darkly but as we are known, we will still never be able to comprehend God in all His fullness. We can now, and will then, worship Him in His greatness. Job needed to repent with regard to his accusations against God. Job's asking the reason for his trials was not so much wonder as it was criticism of God. As long as Job had a question in his heart concerning God's character, he was in no state of mind to have his difficulties met.

We may never get a complete answer this side of glory; but we can have a satisfactory answer so that we can rest with assurance knowing that God knows what He is doing. If we seek our answers in human reason only, we will end

up accusing God. But if we submit ourselves to Him we
will find our rest in Him.

I have been thrilled time and again in reading the
last verses of the 11th chapter of Romans. In Romans 9, 10,
and 11 the Apostle Paul showed how God had dealt with
Israel in the past, how He is dealing with them in the
present, and how He will deal with them in the future.
And so wonderful are God's works in this way that Paul
ended that great section with a most remarkable doxology.
He cried, "O the depth of the riches both of the wisdom
and knowledge of God! how unsearchable are his judgments, and his ways past finding out! For who hath known
the mind of the Lord? or who hath been his counsellor?
Or who hath first given to him, and it shall be recompensed
unto him again? For of him, and through him, and to him,
are all things: to whom be glory for ever. Amen" (11:33-36).

Although God is infinitely above man and entirely
beyond man's comprehension, God is not indifferent to
the needs of His creatures. He is not indifferent to our
problems and heartaches. Neither is He arbitrary in any
way in His dealing with us. Furthermore, He is not neutral.
He is on our side and is seeking our best in all that He
permits to come into our lives.

The Book of Lamentations is a good book to read from
time to time. I have received much benefit from it at
various periods. Here is a fruitful portion from chapter 3:
"For the Lord will not cast off for ever: But though he
cause grief, yet will he have compassion according to the
multitude of his mercies. For he doth not afflict willingly
[that is with pleasure] nor grieve the children of men"
(vv. 31-33).

God is righteous and holy. The Psalmist said of Him
in Psalm 119:75: "I know, O Lord, that thy judgments are
right, and that thou in faithfulness hast afflicted me."
David was a man who saw many afflictions but he attributed
them to God's faithfulness. Some of David's afflictions were

earned by his misconduct. Others again were permitted as were Job's affliction for refining. But in all of them David ascribed faithfulness to God.

Submission to God

It is a principle of God's dealing with us that when we become subject to Him and admit He has some wise purpose in view, He will bring assurance to the heart and take us through to victory.

This was what Elihu set out to explain to Job. Allowing afflictions to come to His children is one of God's ways of dealing with them. Elihu did not assure Job that he would be healed if he recognized this fact but asserted that this was one of God's methods. As long as Job accused God he would receive no answer from Him. But the moment he would submit, God would make it plain. Do we face this problem also? Have we been passing through trials and questioned God's goodness because we saw that our neighbors, whom we felt were not as good as we, had escaped affliction?

God has two ways of speaking with us. One is through the still small voice of the Word of God. The Psalmist said in Psalm 119:9,11: "Wherewithal shall a young man cleanse his way? by taking heed thereto according to thy word. . . . Thy word have I hid in mine heart, that I might not sin against thee." God wants His Word to get into our hearts so that He can speak to us through it. But if the Word is not heeded then God has to speak with the rod.

Listen again to the Psalmist: "Before I was afflicted I went astray: but now have I kept thy Word. . . . It is good for me that I have been afflicted; that I might learn thy statutes" (Ps. 119:67,71). This expresses total submission on the part of the Psalmist. He admitted that if he had not been afflicted he would have gone astray. The Psalmist saw it. But at this place in our study in the Book of Job, Job had not seen it.

Job's three friends had been blunt and harsh. They had said in effect: "Now Job, you are a hypocrite. You have been doing wrong here so you should confess your terrible sins to God. It is because of them that you have been undergoing all these afflictions."

Elihu's approach, as we have seen, was different. He said, "Job, where you have been wrong is that you have been expecting something of God that He does not have to give you. He does not have to answer you. He is greater than you. You must also recognize that God has a purpose in allowing these things to come to your life. So submit yourself to Him. You have not been guilty of the kind of sins your friends have insinuated, but there is pride and lack of submission to God. Give God His rightful place. Acknowledge that He is God. Recognize that you are a mere creature and submit yourself to His wonderful grace."

Here are more of Elihu's words: "He looks upon other men and sings out to them, I have sinned and perverted that which was right, and it did not profit me, but He did not requite me [according to my iniquity]! [The penitent's song continues] God has redeemed my life from going down to the pit of destruction, and I shall see the light of life! [Elihu comments] Lo, God does all these things twice, yes, three times with a man; To bring back his life from the pit of destruction, that he may be enlightened with the light of the living. Give heed, O Job, listen to me; hold your peace, and I will speak. If you have anything to say, answer me; speak, for I desire to justify you. If you do not [have anything to say], listen to me; hold your peace, and I will teach you wisdom" (33:27-33). The Book of Proverbs tells us that the man who covers his sins will not prosper (28:13). But whoever confesses them and forsakes them shall find mercy. Elihu appealed to Job to see his real problem which lay in accusing God instead of justifying Him.

Job had no answer to this. We would judge that his

silence is an acknowledgment that Elihu had spoken truth and presented it clearly to him.

It is not uncommon for us to receive letters in which Christians say that they have sinned and confessed it to God but God will not forgive them. We must never accuse God like that. He says in I John 1:9: "If we confess our sins, he is faithful and just to forgive us our sins, and to cleanse us from all unrighteousness." He said so, therefore we must believe it. Let us not accuse God falsely.

But some come back with the statement that they "don't feel like they've been forgiven." The Lord did not say we would feel like it. He simply says that if we confess He will forgive. Things can affect our feeling such as not being up to par physically or it may be depression brought on by the Evil One. We must not pay attention to our feelings but depend entirely on God's Word. Since God said it, that settles it.

Elihu's argument in the 33rd chapter is that God's government with man is both sovereign and gracious. He takes up another subject in chapter 34 and emphasizes the fact that God's government is righteous and impartial. It cannot be anything else. "Therefore hear me, you men of understanding; far be it from God that He should do wickedness, and from the Almighty that He should commit iniquity. For according to the deeds of a man God will (exactly) proportion his pay, and cause every man to find recompense according to his ways. Truly God will not do wickedly, neither will the Almighty pervert justice" (34: 10,11,12).

God Is Righteous

Elihu gave five reasons why God's government cannot be anything other than righteous and impartial. First of all, God is righteous. God being God will not pervert judgment. God is not a despot sitting somewhere on a throne, finding pleasure in watching people suffer. God as to His nature is love. He is full of compassion for those who have placed their faith in Him. In fact His compassion reaches beyond that by the very fact that He gave Christ to die for all men while they were yet sinners. This is an assurance that He will not withhold any good thing from those who place their faith in Christ. God is perfect and cannot so much as think evil, much less act evil. Nor is He the author of anything wrong in us or in others. James 1:13 says, "Let no man say when he is tempted, I am tempted of God: for God cannot be tempted with evil, neither tempteth he any man."

The Apostle John dealt with the same truth when he wrote: "This then is the message which we have heard of him, and declare unto you, that God is light, and in him is no darkness at all" (I John 1:5). God not only lives in the light but He is the source of light. There is no darkness in Him or about Him. Light here speaks of righteousness and darkness speaks of evil. God could not commit an act of sin in any way. God cannot lie. He cannot do wrong. Neither can He deny Himself. But all good things He can do because He is God.

His dealings with man must of necessity be perfect and just.

God's Care for His Own

In the second place, God is righteous because of His wonderful care of His children. This is something that has been proved time and again. "Who put God in charge over the earth? Or who laid on Him the whole world? If God should withdraw His life-giving spirit and His breath [from men], and cause His heart to return to Himself or set His heart only upon Himself, All flesh would perish together, and man turn again to dust" (Job 34:13-15).

This is telling us that God is the source of all life. All life is in Him. If God for one moment should withdraw His life from any of us we would cease to be. We would pass into nothingness and so would this world. This universe would pass away. God cares for us. This is why He does not withdraw His life from us.

God is Great

In the third place, God is righteous because of His greatness. It is hard for man to describe this greatness. "If now you have understanding, hear this; listen to my words. Is it possible that an enemy of right should govern? And will you condemn Him Who is just and mighty? God Who says to a king, You are worthless and vile, or to princes and nobles, You are ungodly and evil? God is not partial to princes, nor does He regard the rich more than the poor, for they all are the work of His hands. In a moment they die; even at midnight the people are shaken and pass away, and the mighty are taken away by no human hand" (34:16-20).

All things are in God's hands—whether it is the government or the people, the king or the subject. God does not have favorites. A man's station in life makes no difference to God.

One thing man has not overcome and that is death. In fact, he never will overcome it. Man has never been able to create life, for this too is in the hands of God. No wonder the Bible describes Him as the Great God.

Corroboration of this is given in John 1:3-5: "All things were made by him; and without him was not anything made that was made. In him was life; and the life was the light of men. And the light shineth in darkness; and the darkness comprehendeth it not." That is, the darkness cannot overshadow the light. Whenever the light comes, the darkness flees.

Further testimony of God's greatness is given in John 5:26: "For as the Father hath life in himself; so hath he given to the Son to have life in himself." And in his first letter, John says: "He that hath the Son hath life; and he that hath not the Son of God hath not life" (I John 5:12).

God is the source of all life. He creates everything. Anything that has life has received its life from Him. This life is in the Son, and those who have the Son have life. So we who have Christ as Saviour have the life that God gives.

Can we consider Him to be fickle? Can we look on Him and think He is unfair?

God Is All-Wise

In the fourth place, He is righteous because He is all-wise. He knows everything. "For God's eyes are upon the ways of a man, and He sees all his steps. There is no darkness nor thick gloom where the evildoers may hide themselves. God sets before man no appointed time that he should appear before Him in judgment" (34:21-23).

God has perfect discernment. He knows the end from the beginning. He knows how or when to afflict so that the outcome will be just what He desires.

There was no real basis for Job wanting to argue with God or bring his case before Him. God knew all things but Job did not. We do not understand all things but God knows every truth from every angle. He never has to ascertain the facts. He knows them. And it is on the basis of what He knows that He works.

Some of God's works may seem mysterious but He knows what He is doing. Part of the mystery lies in our lack of knowledge; but a good deal of it lies in the fact that we are merely human beings. God raises men to high places or deposes them according to what He knows is best. He overturns the wicked in a night and they are crushed. Because they turn aside from God and have no regard for His ways, He brings them to a swift end. And if God should decide to hide Himself, who can make Him reveal Himself?

Unless we recognize that God knows what He is doing, and believe as Paul tells us that all things work together for good to them that love the Lord, to them that are called according to His purpose, then life will be bitter for us like it was for Job until he learned this lesson.

If we lose faith in God's righteousness what is there left? We might as well do as Job's wife advised him to do, and that was to give up and commit suicide. But this is not the way we look at things because this is not the way God does things. God is righteous and His purposes have not only a good goal in mind but a perfect goal.

To do otherwise is to walk in the counsel of the ungodly. And this is often more dangerous than outward forms of outbreaking evil. It is saying, in effect, there is no profit in seeking peace with God. The opposite is true. There is peace with God.

God's Works Are Righteous

The fifth reason is that every action and work of God proves He is righteous. Even His works of judgment help establish His righteousness. He smites evildoers who depart from Him. He remembers the cause of the poor and needy. He gives life and quietness. These were Elihu's reasons for asserting the righteousness of God.

God's Righteous Judgments

The last point Elihu made was that God is righteous because of His judgments, that is by the way He judges men. We are told that He "strikes them down as wicked men in the open sight of beholders" (34:26). The reason is that "they turned aside from Him, and would not consider or show regard for any of His ways" (v. 27). They oppressed the poor and the poor cried because of their afflictions and God heard them and judged the evildoers.

God also gives quietness, that is, peace and security from oppression: "Who then can condemn and make trouble?" (v. 29). No one can shake that peace. We have referred to this before and pointed out that when God justifies there is none who can condemn. God can strip the godless man of his rulership or keep him from coming to the throne in the first place. He can deal with a nation just as easily as He deals with an individual. In fact, the nations are but a drop in a bucket in His sight. God, not men, is in control in their affairs. He has the final say.

Elihu appealed to Job to accept the lesson that God was teaching him. His words are, "For has any one said to God, I have borne my chastisement, I will not offend any more; Teach me what I do not see [in regard to how I have sinned]; if I have done iniquity, I will do it no more" (vv. 31,32).

Though Elihu was not harsh he did not mince words. He continued in his discourse: "Should [God's] recompense [for your sins] be as you will it, that you refuse to accept it? For you must do the choosing and not I. Therefore say what is your truthful conclusion" (v. 33). Was Job to be the judge of how God should deal with him? He had accused God and harbored wrong thoughts in his heart concerning God's dealing with him. He had found fault with God's judgment because they did not fit into his shortsighted expectations.

Is not this the way we also feel and think when we are in times of difficulty or stress? Haven't we said at times, "If this is the way God is going to deal with me I want nothing to do with Him?" Perhaps we had not gone as far as that, but we have been resentful or questioned God's wisdom and justice in these things.

Elihu told Job that he had spoken without knowledge, consequently his words were without wisdom. He had failed to realize that God is greater than man and that God is never in the wrong. Job's thoughts had been self-centered rather than God-centered. It was for this reason that resentment had built up within him.

Elihu's hope was that these trials through which Job

had passed would bring him to the end of himself and cause him to turn to the Lord for his help. Elihu said: "Would that Job's afflictions be continued and he be tried to the end, because of his answering like wicked men! For he adds rebellion [in his unsubmissive, defiant attitude toward God] to his unacknowledged sin; he claps his hands [in open mockery and contempt of God] among us, and he multiplies his words of accusation against God" (34:36,37). Thank God, Job eventually did see this and came clean for the Lord. That we will see later.

Elihu's Insights

Elihu had summarized their arguments, but his answer was new and distinctive to what had been given by the three friends and even by Job himself. He saw the superior purpose God had in allowing suffering to come to a child of His who was acknowledged to be a good man. The three friends had each accused Job of being guilty of gross sin of one kind or another because, according to their viewpoint, no man would suffer as he had suffered unless he had done something very evil. They thought of suffering as punishment, and when Job refused to accept their judgment, they called him a hypocrite.

Elihu points out that Job's problem and sin was a wrong attitude toward God and toward God's judgments. Job had failed to see that even a good man needs refining in God's school of practical Christian living. Elihu saw that suffering is not exclusively punitive, it may also be corrective. He saw that God allows suffering not always as a penal matter but for moral ends. Suffering is not necessarily to requite a man for sin but to bring a man to an even closer fellowship with God. It may not be for punishment at all but rather for purification. It is not necessarily the Judge's rod of punishment but the Shepherd's crook to guide us. It is something designed to push us a little further on in maturing our spiritual lives.

Elihu saw that through suffering man is restrained from further evil. This is good, for God sees what is ahead though we do not. And it is very possible that trials through which we pass in the present are designed to keep us on the right pathway and stop us from entering the wrong one. Do we not pray in the Lord's Prayer: "Lead us not into temptation, but deliver us from evil"? In so doing we are asking the Lord to keep us out of the place where we will be enticed into committing sin. So in both the Old Testament and the New we learn that chastening is for our good. Through it God develops our character in Christian things and brings us more into the likeness of Christ.

Elihu brought out another factor in God's discipline of His children when he stated in Job 36: "He delivers the afflicted in and by their afflictions, and opens their ears [to His voice] in and by adversity. Indeed, God would have allured you out of the mouth of distress into a broad place where there is no situation of perplexity or privation, and that which would be set on your table would be full of fatness" (vv. 15,16). This takes us a step farther in the matter of afflictions. There is deliverance through them and there is a greater spiritual alertness that comes to us as a result of them. Our ears are opened to where we can hear God speak to us better. But more than that, God seeks to bring us out of our distresses so as to get us into the place where He can fully bless us. He describes this as the broad place where there is a table set full of fatness.

Elihu pointed out to Job that if he would bow before God in these things, sooner or later his sufferings would end. If he remained stubborn, the only recourse was for God to chasten him further.

He then asked Job if in view of all these arguments he considered himself better qualified than God to decide such matters. At one place in his discourse Elihu asked Job if God's dealings with him should be according to Job's desires or thoughts, but Job refused to answer that question.

Apparently he had come to realize that Elihu was dealing with a phase of the subject that he himself had not considered.

Then Elihu brought a strong appeal for Job to submit to God rather than to keep on rebelling in his heart against the afflictions as though they were unrighteous punishments.

Need of a Right Attitude

Elihu put his finger on Job's attitude as the root of Job's trouble. Job had been crying out for God to make Himself known, but his own heart attitude had kept God from this. Apparently this is what Elihu had in mind when he said: "Because of the multitudes of oppressions the people cry out; they cry for help because of the violence of the mighty. But no one says, Where is God my Maker, Who gives songs of rejoicing in the night, Who teaches us more than the beasts of the earth, and makes us wiser than the birds of the heavens? The people cry out because of the pride of evil men, but He does not answer. Surely God will refuse to answer [the cry which is] vanity—vain and empty [instead of abiding trust]; neither will the Almighty regard it" (35:9-13). God searches out men's hearts and when he finds their attitudes and motives are right, He can work on their behalf.

This matter of a right attitude is touched on a number of times throughout the Word of God. We read in Proverbs 16:2: "All the ways of a man are clean in his own eyes; but the Lord weigheth the spirits." We all tend to come to our own rescue and justify ourselves when we are in difficulties. But God does not listen to our words; He examines our hearts. When these are right, He can help us.

Then in Proverbs 17:3 we learn: "The refining pot is for silver, and the furnace for gold: but the Lord trieth the hearts." He will do this through His Word. Hebrews 4:12 in the Amplified is very vivid in connection with what the Word can do: "For the Word that God speaks is alive and full of power—making it active, operative, energizing and effective; it is sharper than any two-edged sword, penetrating to the dividing line of the breath of life (soul) and [the immortal] spirit, and of joints and marrow [that is, of the deepest parts of our nature] exposing and sifting and analyzing and judging the very thoughts and purposes of the heart." But if we will not listen to the Word, God has to send afflictions in order to open our ears and hearts to what He has told us in His Word.

Jeremiah wrote on the same subject when he stated in his great prophecy: "I the Lord search the heart, I try the reins, even to give every man according to his ways, and according to the fruit of his doings" (17:10).

So it is a very practical question that we can ask with regard to Job. How can he hope to receive an answer from God if he insists that God cannot be found? Or how will God answer if He cannot be approached? or if He treats Job like an enemy? These are the things Job had been saying about God. It is no wonder that Elihu states Job had not learned by affliction. And in not learning by affliction he had displayed the same attitude toward God as the wicked did. This was why he was still suffering. So Elihu warned: "Because there is wrath, beware lest you be led away by your sufficiency, and wrath entice you into scorning chastisements; and let not the greatness of the ransom [the suffering, if rightly endured] turn you aside. . . . Take heed, turn not to iniquity, for this [the iniquity of complaining against God] you have chosen rather than [submission in] affliction" (Job 36:18-21).

Elihu warned Job that if he kept on in the path he had chosen his afflictions could lead to physical death. This reminds us of the New Testament teaching concerning the sin unto death of I John 5:16 and I Corinthians 11:30. This is a judgment that falls upon certain believers who persist in a certain expression of obstinate rebellion against God.

Elihu appealed to Job to have a new attitude toward

his afflictions. His so-called friends harped on some wickedness in Job's past. But in this they were wrong. Elihu was concerned with the wrong attitude Job was then expressing. He accepted Job's plea of innocence with regard to the charges of his friends; however, he pointed out that Job's present attitude was wrong. But he also pointed out that God intended these afflictions for Job's good, but they would not have that desired result if Job persisted in his present attitude against God.

He pled with Job to be teachable. He exhorted him to be humble before God and to let God speak to his heart and life. No matter how earnest Job's protestations were to God and to man, they sprang from the wrong motive and wrong thought. In his pride Job thought he knew better than God; and when a man is in such a state of heart God cannot commune with him.

Elihu then questioned Job as to his knowledge of God's greatness. Job was not a novice in these matters, but Elihu tried to get him to think of God from a different angle. He not only showed the wondrous works of God but showed how impossible it is for man to explain them. Neither can man do what God did. Then how should weak man address such a great Being? Here are some of Elihu's arguments: "Hear this, O Job; stand still and consider the wondrous works of God. Do you know how God lays His command upon them, and causes the light or the lightning of His [storm] cloud to shine? Do you know how the clouds are balanced and poised [in the heavens], the wonderful works of Him Who is perfect in knowledge? Or why your garments are hot and dry when He quiets the earth [in sultry summer] with the oppressive south wind? Can you along with Him spread out the sky, which is strong as a molten mirror? Tell us [Job] with what words of man we may address such a Being; we cannot state our case because we are in the dark [in the presence of the unsearchable God]" (37:14-19).

In the second place, Elihu appealed for submissive

patience on the part of Job. God's judgments are not arbitrary but proceed from His absolute understanding.
Therefore God knew all about Job and his friends. God
knew the end from the beginning. So Elihu pleaded with
Job to submit himself in patience recognizing what God
does is right. Since God is resistless as Job himself had
argued, then why resist Him? It would be better to wait
patiently for God and learn what He had to say and do.

In the third place, Elihu appealed to Job to have faith
in God's goodness. It was not enough to believe that God
is. Men must believe that God in His character is righteous
and holy. Rather than demanding an explanation from
Him as to why He does certain things, it is for man to wait
on God's time to reveal His purposes.

Therefore it is necessary that men give God reverence.

In concluding his discourse, Elihu said, "Touching the
Almighty, we cannot find Him out; He is excellent in power,
and to justice and plenteous righteousness He does no
violence—He will disregard no right. Men therefore (reverently) fear Him; He regards and respects not any who
are wise in their own understanding and conceit" (37:23,24).

In this Elihu has risen to a higher and more spiritual
plane than had Job or any of his friends. The matter was
not closed yet, for God took up the subject where Elihu
left off. *But in different ways Elihu made it plain that Job
was not suffering because of his sinning, but was sinning
because of his suffering.* This is something we can all
easily fall into—and we do the moment we start questioning
God's goodness.

The remedy for this is simply to believe in God and
trust Him for the results. This is far better for us than
any explanation God might give us.

Men have difficulty looking at the light in the sky
after the passing of the storm. How much more difficulty

would they encounter if brought face to face with the glory of God.

God's servant took in hand the spiritual restoration of Job as far as he could do it. Now it was time for God to step in and do what no man could do.

CHAPTER ELEVEN

THE LORD SPEAKS TO JOB

It is apparent that as Elihu was in the midst of his discourse a great storm was in the making. We are not told how long he spoke, but his frequent references to the great thunderclouds, the flashing of the lightning, and the pouring down of the rain, form a background for many of his statements and arguments toward the end of his speech.

For example he says according to Job 36:26-33: "Behold! God is great, and we know Him not; the number of His years is unsearchable. For He draws up the drops of water, which distil in rain from His vapor, Which the skies pour down and drop abundantly upon (the multitudes of) mankind. Not only that, but can any one understand the spreadings of the clouds or the thunderings of His pavilion? Behold, He spreads His lightning against the dark clouds, and covers the roots of the sea. For by His clouds God executes judgment upon the peoples; He gives food in abundance. He covers His hands with light or the lightning, and commands it against the assailant and to strike the mark."

Here Elihu showed how impossible it is for us to explain God. Our knowledge of Him is fragmentary. In the words of Paul, "We see through a glass darkly." We need as believers to submit to God rather than to try to reason out the ways of God.

Who can really understand God? This was what Elihu

asked Job, and this is a question asked again and again in the Scriptures. Isaiah referred to it when he wrote: "Have ye not known? have ye not heard? hath it not been told you from the beginning? have ye not understood from the foundations of the earth? It is he that sitteth upon the circle of the earth, and the inhabitants thereof are as grasshoppers; that stretcheth out the heavens as a curtain, and spreadeth them out as a tent to dwell in: That bringeth the princes to nothing; he maketh the judges of the earth as vanity" (Isa. 40:21-23).

It is worthy of note that the statement concerning God's sitting upon the circle of the earth is a reference to the earth's being round. Our Western World discovered this for itself only a few hundred years ago, yet the fact was written down about seven hundred years before Christ.

This, however, is a small matter compared to the great spiritual truths unfolded: "Hast thou not known? hast thou not heard, that the everlasting God, the Lord, the Creator of the ends of the earth, fainteth not, neither is weary? there is no searching of his understanding. He giveth power to the faint; and to them that have no might he increaseth strength. Even the youths shall faint and be weary, and the young men shall utterly fall: But they that wait upon the Lord shall renew their strength; they shall mount up with wings as eagles; they shall run, and not be weary; and they shall walk, and not faint" (Isa. 40:28-31).

Elihu again referred to the gathering storm when he said in chapter 37: "Indeed, [at His thunderings] my heart also trembles, and leaps out of its place. Hear, oh, hear the roar of His voice and the sound of rumbling that goes out of His mouth! Under the whole heaven He lets it loose, and His lightning to the ends of the earth. After it His voice roars; He thunders with the voice of His majesty, and He restrains not [His lightnings against His adversaries] when His voice is heard. God thunders marvelously with His voice; He does great things which we cannot comprehend. For He says to the snow, Fall on the

earth; likewise He speaks to the showers and to the down-
pour of His mighty rains" (vv. 1-6).

Elihu once more appealed to Job and asked him to
stand still and consider the wondrous works of God: "Do
you know how God lays His command upon them, and
causes the light or the lightning of His [storm] cloud to
shine? Do you know how the clouds are balanced and
poised [in the heavens], the wonderful works of Him
Who is perfect in knowledge?" (vv. 15,16).

The point Elihu made is that since God is so wonderful
in His works how are we to address Him? He is so far
above us in knowledge and in power that we are virtually
in the dark. Our knowledge of the things around us is very
limited. "Touching the Almighty, we cannot find Him out;
He is excellent in power, and to justice and plenteous
righteousness He does no violence—He will disregard no
right. Men therefore (reverently) fear Him; He regards
and respects not any who are wise in their own understanding and conceit" (37:23,24).

The patriarch's so-called friends had failed to help
him because they approached his problem from the wrong
premise. They argued that he was suffering because of
specific sins he had committed. He rejected their viewpoint,
and rightly so. Though they were wrong, God nevertheless
used them, even through their false accusations, to demonstrate in Job the presence of his fallen nature. I know
what this is about, for I have a fallen nature living within
me, too. He is just as old as I am. He cannot be changed
nor can he be trained. He cannot be changed for the better.
He is unchangeably evil, and if I give him room he will
show himself.

This is what happened to Job. His reaction to the false
accusations was not spiritual but carnal. The greatest
enemy we have, showed up in Job and shows up in us when
we provide it with an opening.

Elihu served as a mediator, assuring Job that his friends
were wrong, but pointing out that there were some things

that Job needed to know about himself and about God. Elihu took this line of thought with Job as far as he could and then God began to speak.

Things Happen When God Speaks

It would seem that the storm had reached its peak. The lightning flashed, the thunder rolled and the rain poured down. Out of the midst of this great convulsion in the elements God spoke, and what He said had an immediate effect.

When our first parents heard the voice of the Lord in the Garden of Eden after they had disobeyed Him, they were stricken with guilt and tried to hide themselves from His presence.

Moses heard the voice of God at the burning bush and took off his shoes, for he was standing on holy ground. Later when God spoke to him on Mount Sinai after the deliverance of the children of Israel from Egypt, Moses said, "I exceedingly fear and quake."

Many years later when Elijah the prophet was in a cave on Mount Horeb, the Lord told him to go forth from the cave and stand on the mountain before Him. Then there came a great wind which broke the very rocks, but the Lord was not in the wind. This was followed by a great earthquake, but the Lord was not in the earthquake. Next was fire, but the Lord was not in the fire. Finally there came a still small voice which penetrated the very soul of Elijah. It was after this that he returned to his ministry.

Another time God spoke was when Jesus was baptized. John the Baptist had said some wonderful things about the Lord, and then the Father said from heaven: "This is my beloved Son in whom I am well pleased." This statement ever stands as God's endorsement of His Son and His ministry.

Saul the great persecutor of the Church was on the road to Damascus when he heard a voice from heaven saying, "Saul, Saul, why persecutest thou me?" Saul was a Pharisee, zealous for God, but his zeal was misplaced and was taking him in the wrong direction. The voice from heaven changed his life, his heart, his goal and gave him a ministry in conformity with the will of God.

We read concerning the great endtime judgment which will fall upon the earth when the Lord shall appear to judge the earth: "And the kings of the earth, and the great men, and the rich men, and the chief captains, and the mighty men, and every bondman, and every free man, hid themselves in the dens and in the rocks of the mountains; And said to the mountains and rocks, Fall on us, and hide us from the face of him that sitteth on the throne, and from the wrath of the Lamb: For the great day of his wrath is come; and who shall be able to stand?" (Rev. 6:15-17). When God speaks men listen; everyone pays attention, and things begin to happen.

> When God speaks, the high mountains tremble;
> When God speaks, the loud billows roll;
> When God speaks, my heart falls to list'ning,
> And there is response in my soul.
>
> Speak to my heart!
> Speak now, I pray,
> God of salvation, and Lord of Creation,
> Oh, speak to my heart today.*
>
> —Carlton C. Buck

God's voice brought Job consciously into the very presence of God. This was the God whom heretofore he had not seen and said he could not find. Before this the discussion had been about God. God has been spoken of

---

* © 1936 and 1964, by Lillenas Publishing Company. By permission.

as absent. Now Job was suddenly brought face to face with Him.

Was This Discourse Private?

Did the other four men hear this discourse? The Bible does not say; consequently we dare not be dogmatic about it. But my own feeling in the matter is that it was very much the same with Job as it was with Saul on the way to Damascus. The Lord spoke to Saul, but the men who were with him heard a voice but saw no man (Acts 9:7). They heard the sound of the voice but they did not understand the words. To me it is a wonderful thought that in His reproofs of us, God speaks to us in private. He does not expose a servant of His to mockery and shame before His friends.

Moses spent 40 years of his life in the quiet of the desert away from the teeming cities of Egypt. During those years God was, without doubt, preparing His servant for his great life's work. There would be reproof and counsel, a dealing with Moses in many precious ways, but nothing is said about it. Those 40 years are passed over in just a few sentences. Whatever private dealings God had with Moses are not mentioned with the exception of the incident of the burning bush.

We should be thankful to God that He deals privately with us concerning the faults of our hearts. Suppose He exposed them to everyone and made a mockery of us? What would we think of God then? Even though God may come in the thunder and the lightning as He did to Job, He speaks to us privately.

As I have stated, I have no proof that this was a private conversation, but in the light of God's dealing with others of His servants it would seem to me that this was so.

The word "Lord" in Job 38:1 is Jehovah. This name is rich in meaning and is explained in Exodus chapters 3 and 6. God was known to Moses as the Almighty God until He revealed Himself as the great "I AM." This means the "Ever-present One," the "Becoming One." If Job realized something of the significance of the Name, he would know that the Lord was saying to him, "I will be to you what I am."

Have we learned to know the Lord as the Ever-present One, the great I AM, the One who is ever present with us and will ever fill the need in our hearts and lives?

Elihu had asked Job a question but Job did not answer. This first verse of chapter 38 could be paraphrased in this way: "And Jehovah answered for, or in behalf of, Job." Job had asked God to answer him (31:35). God did, but He not only answered Job but answered Elihu's question in behalf of Job.

Job had let the old or fallen nature have its way for awhile, so it is no wonder he had no answer. He could not and did not try to excuse himself. He could only abhor himself, but this was not his reaction until later.

When Elihu had pressed on Job to give an answer to the things he had discussed, God broke in on the scene and answered for him. How wonderful is our God! This very act upon His part would be enough to break down a man's opposition to God. I am sure it did something for Job. God, whom Job thought could not be reached came to his rescue and answered for him. This is the God we worship and serve.

In God's Presence

When a child of God is suddenly brought into God's presence, there is always a profound effect upon that believer's life. At one time Peter said to Jesus, "Depart from me; for I am a sinful man, O Lord." He suddenly realized that being in the presence of the Lord Jesus, he was in the presence of God.

When the Lord appeared to Saul on the road to Damascus he fell to the ground and cried, "Lord what wilt thou have me to do?"

When the Apostle John on Patmos saw the glorious vision of Christ in His second-coming glory, he fell at Christ's feet as dead. Then we are told that the Lord laid His right hand upon John and said to him: "Fear not; I am the first and the last: I am he that liveth, and was dead; and behold, I am alive forevermore" (Rev. 1:17,18).

Do we realize that the Word of God is nothing else than God speaking to us? God is not merely giving us history through His Word. He Himself speaks through it. When this dawns upon us, the Bible will have a brand-new meaning to us. We will not take it lightly as we may have in the past. There are some who even dare to twist it and change it to suit themselves, but they do so at their own peril. Oh that we might be like the child Samuel who, when he heard God calling him, said, "Speak, Lord, for thy servant heareth."

Job was now on the listening end of things. But he was no longer listening to some men who accused him falsely; he was listening to God whom he had wanted to see and from whom he had asked for an answer.

Job had to see himself but he could only see himself in the right way when he saw God. The things that were hidden deep down in Job's heart were not made plain to him until God brought them to the surface. Our outward actions may deceive others, but our inner reactions tell what we really are. This is why God looks on the heart. He does not see as man sees: "For man looketh on the outward appearance, but the Lord looketh on the heart" (I Sam. 16:7). Job was brought face to face with God so that he might also be brought face to face with himself.

The arguments Job made when he was falsely accused were not repeated when Elihu addressed him. Job was brought face to face with some of the ugly things in his own heart and was silenced. Now God was able to speak to him.

Later on Job was brought to the end of himself and admitted that he had nothing more to say. His attitude toward God was transformed when he admitted he had heard of God but now he saw Him and, therefore, he abhorred himself and repented in dust and ashes.

Now that God has begun His dealing with Job, will He rebuke and reprove him for what he has said? Will God touch his body and heal it? Will Job's losses be restored?

Job's Spiritual Need

Perhaps we are disappointed that God did not immediately move to restore Job in these ways. God did not even argue with him. Why should He? Instead, He asked Job a series of questions which were designed to bring him to right thinking and right believing.

Job had shown some arrogance. He needed to be humbled. In this God used irony to good effect. There was no sarcasm included, for God's purpose was not to humiliate Job but to produce humbleness of heart in him. It is one thing to be brought to the place where we recognize we are nothing; it is quite another to be so bullied or made fun of or made to look cheap that we inwardly cringe at the treatment we receive. This last is not humility but humiliation. Men can easily humiliate each other, but it takes God to humble us. This is a vital distinction to know.

The scientists sweep the heavens with their telescopes. They pierce the heart of the secret things of the earth with their microscopes. Then they talk learnedly, even interestingly, about "the laws of nature" and "the principles of chemistry and physics," of "gravitation," "cohesion," and many other things. They have even discovered some of the inner power of God's creation in the atom. But unless the scientist has heard the voice of God, he does not know the significance of the truth he sees nor does he know God Himself.

This ignorance is a guilty ignorance. God will not excuse it, for man has no excuse when he fails to see in nature the evidences of God's power and greatness.

This is the very thing Paul warns of in Romans 1:18-25: "For the wrath of God is revealed from heaven against all ungodliness and unrighteousness of men, who hold the truth in unrighteousness; Because that which may be known of God is manifest in them; for God hath shewed it unto them. For the invisible things of him from the creation of the world are clearly seen, being understood by the things that are made, even his eternal power and Godhead; so that they are without excuse: Because that, when they knew God, they glorified him not as God, neither were thankful; but became vain in their imaginations, and their foolish heart was darkened. Professing themselves to be wise, they became fools, And changed the glory of the uncorruptible God into an image made like to corruptible man, and to birds, and fourfooted beasts, and creeping things. Wherefore God also gave them up to uncleanness through the lusts of their own hearts, to dishonour their own bodies between themselves: Who changed the truth of God into a lie, and worshipped and served the creature more than the Creator, who is blessed for ever. Amen."

In dealing with Job, however, God did not speak in great theological terms nor develop great theological truths. He questioned Job to find out if he knew the truths that lie open to eyes that will see in God's vast creation around us. He did not speak in a language that no man can understand but in the language of nature. God spoke of the earth, the sky, the clouds, the rain, the beasts and birds. It is true that we cannot comprehend God, but His creation can give us something that shows His eternal power and Godhead. We can reason from what we know to the unknown. We can see that God is far above His creation.

Such truth can also bring us to see what we are, and this, in turn brings us to the end of ourselves.

God veils His glory, for He dwells in unapproachable light. Nevertheless, He shows Himself in a measure in the works of His hands. True it is, we see through a glass darkly, but a day is coming when we shall see Him face to face.

God even veiled off His glory when the Lord Jesus Christ came to dwell among us as a man. We learn in Philippians 2:6-11 that Christ "being in the form of God, thought it not robbery to be equal with God: But made himself of no reputation, and took upon him the form of a servant, and was made in the likeness of men: And being found in fashion as a man, he humbled himself, and became obedient unto death, even the death of the cross. Wherefore God also hath highly exalted him, and given him a name which is above every name: That at the name of Jesus every knee should bow, of things in heaven, and things in earth, and things under the earth; And that every tongue should confess that Jesus Christ is Lord, to the glory of God the Father."

Though men did not see Christ in His heavenly glory, His incarnation has provided us with spiritual insight concerning Him that could not have been known had He not lived among us and died and rose again. In the second chapter of Ephesians we read: "And you hath he quickened, who were dead in trespasses and sins: Wherein in time past ye walked according to the course of this world, according to the prince of the power of the air, the spirit that now worketh in the children of disobedience" (Eph. 2:1,2). But even more has been done for us, for we learn a few verses later: "Even when we were dead in sins, hath quickened us together with Christ, (by grace ye are saved;) And hath raised us up together, and made us sit together in heavenly places in Christ Jesus." We belong now in heavenly spheres and have been given a new insight into the spiritual realm.

Job was a godly man but there was something that he had not seen. He did not see his real self nor had he seen God as He is. When God asked Job questions concerning the vast creation around him it was as though He said, "I am Master, Lord of all this." So the questions could really be stated in this way: "Can you doubt the power and wisdom and goodness of One who sends the rain to meet man's needs? Can you doubt the faithfulness of a God who brings His mercies day by day to His creation? Can you doubt God at all?"

Jeremiah went through experiences similar to those of Job. The cases are not exactly parallel but Jeremiah was mistreated. He was given a message to preach and told that his own people would not listen to him, and he would even suffer for telling the truth.

Jeremiah was faithful, but when he was cast into a dungeon and persecuted for doing God's will, he almost despaired. Yet in the midst of his agony of soul he voiced some rich truth. From Lamentations the third chapter we read these following portions. In verses 7 and 8 Jeremiah said, "He hath hedged me about, that I cannot get out: He hath made my chain heavy. Also when I cry and shout, He shutteth out my prayer." Later on in verse 11 he said, "He hath turned aside my ways, and pulled me in pieces: he hath made me desolate." Still further along we read: "I was a derision to all my people; and their song all the day. He hath filled me with bitterness, He hath made me drunken with wormwood. He hath also broken my teeth with gravel stones, he hath covered me with ashes. And thou hast removed my soul far off from peace: I forgat prosperity. And I said, My strength and my hope is perished from the Lord: Remembering mine affliction and my misery, the wormwood and the gall" (Lam. 3:14-19). It was in the midst of this great lament that he expressed this glorious truth: "This I recall to my mind, therefore have I hope. It is of the Lord's mercies that we are not consumed, because his compassions fail not. They are new every morning: great is thy faithfulness. The Lord is my portion, saith my soul; therefore will I hope in him" (vv. 21-24).

Then Jeremiah added: "For the Lord will not cast off for ever: But though he cause grief, yet will he have compassion according to the multitude of his mercies. For he doth not afflict willingly nor grieve the children of men" (vv. 31-33). God does not find pleasure in seeing His children pass through afflictions. He does not take delight in seeing us in sorrow. He permits these things to come to us as measures of discipline with the eventual purpose of spiritual growth in our lives.

God's Purposes

God's next words to Job were, "Who is this that darkeneth counsel by words without knowledge? Gird up now thy loins like a man; for I will demand of thee, and answer thou me" (vv. 2,3, KJV). Job had spoken words that were without knowledge, but now that he was silent, God called on him to lend an attentive ear to what He had to say.

God's method was to expose Job's profound ignorance of His natural government. By this He showed Job's utter incapacity to pass judgment on His moral government which is by far more incomprehensible and mysterious. Job had allowed his fallen nature to direct his words and thoughts to where he said things against God's moral government, things which he later regretted.

God had at least four reasons for appearing to Job at this time and dealing with him as He did.

First of all, it was not God's intention to explain to Job the meaning of his sufferings. Had he been told the purpose of his trial, the good intended would have been nullified. This would have affected his reactions. The trials would not have shown what was deep down in his heart; there would have been no real test of Job's character, no place for faith to be exercised. Yet our faith needs to be tested according to I Peter 1:6,7: "Wherein ye greatly rejoice, though now for a season, if need be, ye are in heaviness through manifold temptations: That the trial of your faith, being much more precious than of gold that perisheth, though it be tried with fire, might be found unto praise and honour and glory at the appearing of Jesus Christ." There is something about our sufferings as believers which God cannot explain to us at the time we are passing through them without destroying the very purposes they are designed to fulfill.

A second purpose is that the fact God talked to Job indicated God was definitely concerned in Job's affairs and had been watching and hearing and caring for this man whom He loved. The songwriter asks and then answers:

> Does Jesus care when my heart is pained
> Too deeply for mirth and song,
> As the burdens press, and the cares distress,
> And the way grows weary and long?

> O yes, He cares, I know He cares.
> His heart is touched with my grief.
> When the days are weary, the long nights dreary,
> I know my Saviour cares.

There is an incident in the life of our Lord which illustrates His compassion for our human griefs. This took place after the death of Lazarus. It tells how our Saviour reacted when He saw the grief of the family and friends: "When Jesus therefore saw her weeping, and the Jews also weeping which came with her, he groaned in the spirit, and was troubled, And said, Where have ye laid him? They said unto him, Lord, come and see. Jesus wept. Then said the Jews, Behold how he loved him!" (John 11:33-36). Lazarus was precious to his sisters, to his friends and above all to the Lord Jesus Himself. Our Saviour mingled His tears with the sorrowing friends and family which shows how deeply God feels about our affairs.

A third purpose God had in dealing with Job as He did was to bring His servant to the point where he rested in God even though he had no explanation for what God was doing. Neither do we need explanations when we know our affairs are in God's hands. It has already been pointed out that one of the questions raised and answered with regard to the Book of Job is, "Can a man serve God simply for what He is and not for what he gets from Him?" This is an equally valid matter for us to consider. God wants us to rest our whole being, our lives, everything about us with complete confidence in Him.

The tests and trials we pass through should bring us to the same place three of the disciples were brought to when our Lord was transformed before them. They were on a mountain with Him when Elijah and Moses appeared and talked to Him. Peter was both excited and frightened by the scene and suggested that he and the other disciples build three tabernacles, one for Elijah, one for Moses, and one for the Lord. Then a cloud overshadowed them and a voice spoke saying, "This is my beloved Son: hear him. And suddenly, when they had looked round about, they saw no man any more, save Jesus only with themselves" (Mark 9:6-8). Here is the purpose for God allowing trials to come into our lives. It is so that we might have a new look at the Lord Jesus. Such situations help us to comprehend Him as He really is.

Faith in the Bible sense is to trust God Himself over against all seeming contradictions and in the absence of all explanations. This is not blind faith, however. Blind faith would be faith without any basis whatsoever. The Scriptures reveal in a large number of incidents that God is faithful and is deeply concerned with our situation.

The fourth reason for the Lord speaking to Job was to bring him to the end of himself. We all have what we call "the old nature," sometimes referred to as "self"; and this nature's power must be broken in our lives. The Lord has provided a remarkable method to accomplish this according to Romans 6. There we are told that we are identified with Christ in His death, and that in His death He annulled the power of this fallen nature. Job did not have that knowledge, but we have though we do not always appropriate it. Through trials we are made aware of our need of finding victory through Christ.

Job needed to be brought to the end of himself, to the end of self-righteousness, self-vindication, self-wisdom —self-everything, so that he might find his all in all in God alone.

Sometimes God allows darkness to come over our hearts in order that we might see Christ only. We are brought to a healthy position when we can say with Paul, "That I may know him, and the power of his resurrection" (Phil. 3:10). This passage was preceded with the statement: "Let this mind be in you, which was also in Christ Jesus: Who, being in the form of God, thought it not robbery to be equal with God: But made himself of no reputation, and took upon him the form of a servant, and was made in the likeness of men: And being found in fashion as a man, he humbled himself, and became obedient unto death, even the death of the cross." The Lord Jesus veiled off His glory when He became man and sometimes God veils off His glory from us so that we may eventually come to see Him as He really is. This is why the Lord said in Luke 9:23: "If any man will come after me, let him deny himself, and take up his cross daily, and follow me."

CHAPTER TWELVE

GOD'S TESTIMONY FROM CREATION

In speaking to Job, God dwelt largely upon His power, wisdom, and goodness as displayed in the works of creation. To this He added His care over them.

In the second place, God showed His power over certain untamable beasts which defy man's authority to control them. With these two distinct approaches He brought Job to the end of himself and to an entirely new understanding of God.

Job had presumed to pass judgment on God's moral government. Job said in so many words that God was not handling the situation correctly. God answered this criticism by testing Job's knowledge with regard to the visible creation. If Job was limited in his knowledge and power over the things he could see, what did he really know about the things he could not see?

How like Job we have been at times. Have we not sat in judgment on God? We have asked, "Why does God do this? Why does God do that? Why doesn't He do this in this manner?" Any approach of this nature, is in reality, our sitting in judgment on God.

Shall the creature so puny in power, ignorant and filled with vain pride, presume to instruct God as to His duties? Are we competent to point out God's failures to Him? Are we right in assuming God's prerogatives? This is what we do when we invade such an area. God allows us to see these things in Job so that we might see them in ourselves.

God questioned His servant in order to bring out two answers. His first answer comes at the end of His first speech. Then it was that Job abased himself and laid his hand upon his mouth. Here is what he said, "Behold I am vile; what shall I answer thee? I will lay mine hand upon my mouth. Once have I spoken; but I will not answer: yea, twice; but I will proceed no further" (Job 40:4,5, KJV).

This was a good response as far as it went. But it was not enough. God continued to deal with His servant until he finally came to the end of himself.

In this second discourse the Lord set before Job creatures in which pride is exhibited. This was designed to bring Job to a place of humbleness. The Lord had in His first words asked Job who it was that darkened counsel by words without knowledge. Then He said, "Gird up now thy loins like a man; for I will demand of thee, and answer thou me." Job had rashly said prior to this that as a prince he would go near to God (31:37). This is only one of the many foolish statements that he later repented of.

Job had poured out a flood of lamentations in protestations and accusations. Much of what he said was true, but it was valueless so far as God's purposes were concerned. It merely served to exalt Job and his own righteousness at the expense of God's righteousness. It is no wonder, then, that God asked who was darkening counsel with words. Was it someone equal to God? Who would be so bold as to lay a charge against his Maker?

Have we not like Job been guilty at times of questioning God's ways with us? Who are we to speak and say that we want nothing to do with a God who allows the things to come into our lives that sometimes appear. A bold and rebellious Lucifer would say such things. Should we act like him?

How differently the Psalmist viewed life. We read: "When I consider thy heavens, the work of thy fingers, the moon and the stars, which thou hast ordained; What is man, that thou art mindful of him? and the son of man, that thou visitest him?" (Ps. 8:3,4). Paul had something to add on this same subject: "Nay but, oh man, who art thou that repliest against God? Shall the thing formed say to him that formed it, Why hast thou made me thus?" (Rom. 9:20). Shall man, a finite, fallible, fallen creature, be more just than his Maker? God writes this great question over all the books and the speeches of men whether they are scientists, historians or philosphers when they willfully exclude His revelation.

God appealed both to the reason and to the conscience of Job. He told him to answer as a man would answer. He took him to the vast yet familiar scenes of creation with which Job had evidenced some knowledge. But could Job answer some of the ten thousand riddles that face men in these things? Could he open the secrets of nature? The evolutionary theory is the unbeliever's attempt to answer where we came from, but it makes a god out of "chance" and leaves man without a reason for being.

Seven Major Aspects of Creation

In questioning Job God presents seven major aspects of His creation and asks Job about each one of them. The questions in some respects are very simple and a college student with some knowledge of geology, physical geography and astronomy might not hestitate to give answers to them. We consider ourselves much advanced in knowledge over Job and his day. Nevertheless, if God were left out, the answers would be superficial and would bog down in the mire of human speculation. Socrates is credited with saying, "All human knowledge is but a knowledge of our ignorance."

As I thought on these matters concerning my own life,

I could not help but say, "Oh God, You have control over every aspect of Your creation. Why is it You can't have complete control over me?" The answer of course is obvious: it is my own personal rebellion. Man was made in the image of God, made to choose either to do the will of God or not. He is the only one of earth's creatures who can so choose. But when it is a believer who is involved, God, because He is sovereign, has ways and means of producing obedience.

This was Job's situation and this is the goal to which God was directing him.

The key to all the questions God asked Job was God Himself. When we know Him, we know the Source and Author of all knowledge. Leave Him out of the picture and all the findings of science leave us at a blank wall beyond which still lies hidden truth. If we would examine ourselves by these same questions, we would end up admitting that God is God. So why not let God be God in our lives now? He is the All-wise, the Almighty, the All-righteous One. Without Him we would fade into nothingness, just as a sunbeam suddenly disappears when the sunlight is cut off.

The Earth

The first of these great questions begins in 38:4: "Where were you when I laid the foundation of the earth? Declare, if you have and know understanding. Who determined the measures of the earth, if you know? Or who stretched the measuring line upon it? Upon what were the foundations of it fastened, or who laid its corner stone, When the morning stars sang together, and all the sons of God shouted for joy?" (vv. 4-7).

God's first question begins with the earth, man's dwelling place. Does Job know the history of his own abode? Where was he when the Great Architect laid the foundations? These were not placed upon shifting sands or solid rock but in empty space where there is apparent nothingness. Where are these foundations? Present-day knowledge talks learnedly about nebulas and the solar system and of the attraction of the law of gravity. It tries to explain the reciprocal action of all these laws as having given the earth its form and stability and its stable relation with other heavenly bodies. Men speak knowingly of the laws of cohesion and of chemical affinity so that the particles of the earth cleave together. These things science tells us as it speaks of the laws of nature, but we must remember that where there are laws there has to be a lawgiver.

Who established these laws? How is it they act so unfailingly? These were questions asked Job and they are asked of us today. This includes the scientific world. If the answer is some form of evolution, then the person giving such an answer only demonstrates his ignorance. Even though I am not a scientist, I have no hesitancy in saying this, for I believe God and believe that He is the Creator as He says. God will put men's answers to the test, and those men who give the wrong answers will have to stand and see themselves proved wrong one of these days.

In Hebrews 12:26,27 God tells us that He is going to shake the earth and the heaven in such a way that only the unshakable things will remain. All of man's learning and ideas will be tested. Only what is according to truth will stand. This means, of course, that only the real knowledge of God together with that which He has created will stand in that day.

We are told in John 1:3 that all things were made by Christ and without Him was not anything made that was made. Then Paul in Colossians 1:17 adds these thoughts: "And he is before all things, and by him all things consist [hold together]." There is no other answer to this question that God raises. The word "nature" is used by men to describe the material and physical world, but it is often used to hide man's unbelief in God. Yet where can the laws of nature lead us but back to God Himself?

When someone substitutes the evolutionary theory for God, he marks himself as a rebel against God. The theory is not compatible with the clearly revealed facts of Scripture that state God is Creator. I say it with all kindness but also with firmness, that there is no future but hell for those who reject God in the face of what nature and the laws of nature reveal. God is back of these laws and controls them.

The earth depends on God for its creation and its continuation. He is its foundation. In the spiritual realm this is equally true for we read concerning salvation: "Other foundation can no man lay than that is laid, which is Jesus Christ" (I Cor. 3:11). There is no other foundation for salvation. Many people have religion, even a so-called Christian religion, but because they do not have Christ they have no foundation. It also means they have no salvation.

As far as this physical world and its laws and its foundation are concerned they all go back to God Himself. He has made certain laws by which the earth hangs in space. To our way of looking at it, it seems to hang on nothing, yet it is stable and remains where God put it. God has so devised nature that an honest examination of it will cause us to look beyond it to Him. But nature itself can only point to His eternal power and Godhead. We need the Bible to tell us more. What we know about God's earth and its origin makes us realize the vast ocean of our ignorance. The light we have exposes the intensity of the darkness that surrounds us.

The physical is typical of the moral and spiritual. Would we question God's physical laws? There are many who are scientists who also are Bible believers. On the other hand there are many scientists who do not acknowledge God at all though they do not question the existence of physical laws.

God points out that the physical laws lead us on to the subject of moral laws. If God can provide physical laws so that everything in the universe functions as it should, can He not also make moral laws and spiritual laws so that human beings will behave as they should? A lawgiver for physical laws argues for a Moral Governor of the universe.

The testings Job endured and the testings we face as believers are all designed to bring us closer to God. Then why do we rebel against God when testings come?

I often visit friends in hospitals. Though I sympathize with them, I must admit that I do not know from experience what they are passing through. There are many kinds of suffering and I have had my share, but physical suffering that requires hospitalization is something I have not experienced. Nevertheless, I know that suffering, regardless of its nature, is used of God for the benefit of our spiritual lives.

Job was left speechless in the face of this question. And if we would be frank, we would be speechless also. So let us bow our knee and let God be God in our lives.

The Sea

The second question the Lord asks is in Job 38:8-11: "Or who shut up the sea with doors, when it broke forth and issued out of the womb? When I made clouds the garment of it, and thick darkness a swaddling band for it, And marked and broke out for it My appointed boundary, and set bars and doors, And said, Thus far shall you come and no farther, and here shall your proud waves be stayed?"

Here God passes from the subject of the land to the sea. There are a number of related questions with regard to this. The first has reference to the earth and the sea in their original form as described in Genesis 1. The earth was waste and empty and darkness was on the face of the deep. It is possible the Scriptures are speaking here of a judgment that came on the original creation. A little later in the chapter we read of the re-creative days when God separated the waters from the land.

The sea and its power and majesty are subjects touched on in a number of the Psalms. In Psalm 33:7 we read: "He gathereth the waters of the sea together as an heap: he layeth up the depth in storehouses." Then in Psalm 89:9 the Psalmist says, "Thou rulest the raging of the sea: when the waves thereof arise, thou stillest them." Again, in Psalm 93:4 we find this: "The Lord on high is mightier than the noise of many waters, yea, than the mighty waves of the sea."

When my wife and I visited Brazil our hotel was on the shore of the Atlantic Ocean. We saw the waves from our room and we could hear them all night long. We saw them as we walked along the beach. They would come roaring and rushing toward us as though saying, "I'm going to engulf you." But they held no fear for us because we knew that God had set bounds for them.

God used water at the beginning to cover the earth in judgment; then again at the time of Noah He judged the earth with water. Man could not then and cannot today control the powers of the great oceans. They show him his helplessness and his ignorance. Only God can control the powers of the seas.

Jeremiah remarked on this subject. He wrote: "Fear ye not me? saith the Lord: will ye not tremble at my presence, which have placed the sand for the bound of the sea by a perpetual decree, that it cannot pass it: and though the waves thereof toss themselves, yet can they not prevail; though they roar, yet can they not pass over it?" (Jer. 5:22). God is in control of the elements. They have no choice but to obey Him.

There is an ocean of evil around us made up of the

pride of Satan and the pride of evil men. This bursts forth in rebellion against God, and at times it looks as if it might take over; but God's restraining hand holds it all in check. Then there is a day coming when He will judge this system of evil. Though the wicked, like the foaming sea, seem to rise higher and higher in violence and pride, God says to them as He does to the physical waves: "Hitherto shalt thou come, but no farther."

Can God control our evil hearts? Even we who have turned to Christ in faith for salvation find there is an evil power within us that we cannot control. This was Paul's dilemma according to Romans 7. He cried out for help and God assured him that Jesus Christ would free him. (See Rom. 7:24,25; 8:2-4.)

In the new heaven and in the new earth there will be no more sea. Sin will also be confined, for those men who will have died as rebels against God will be confined for eternity in the lake of fire.

God wants control over us now. Does He have it?

God's interrogations are very penetrating. He had a specific purpose in questioning Job. Here are some of those questions as we find them in Job 38:4-39:20 (KJV): "Where wast thou when I laid the foundations of the earth? Who hath laid the measures thereof? Whereupon are the foundations thereof fastened? Hast thou commanded the morning since thy days? Hast thou entered into the springs of the sea? or hast thou walked in the search of the depth? Hast thou perceived the breadth of the earth? Where is the way where light dwelleth? Knowest thou it, because thou wast then born? Hast thou entered into the treasures of the snow? Canst thou bind? Canst thou bring forth? Knowest thou the ordinances of heaven? Canst thou set the dominion thereof in the earth? Canst thou lift up thy voice to the clouds? Canst thou send lightning? Wilt thou hunt the prey for the lion? Knowest thou the time when the wild goats of the rock bring forth? Canst thou number the months that they fulfil? Wilt thou trust him? Wilt thou believe him, that he will bring home thy seed? Hast thou given the horse his strength? Canst thou make him afraid as a grasshopper?

It would be good for us if we were to be questioned like that. In fact these are written down that we might consider them. They were not only given for Job's benefit but also for ours. If we cannot answer these questions adequately, then we are in no position to raise any questions about God's handling of the moral laws of the universe.

Day and Night

The third major line of questions concerning God's creation has to do with the daily matter of day and night or light and darkness. The Lord said, "Have you commanded the morning since your days began, and caused the dawn to know its place, So that light may get hold of the corners of the earth and shake the wickedness [of night] out of it?" (38:12,13). The Lord is simply asking Job if he had ever commanded a single morning to appear or caused the dawn to appear in the right place. Suppose the sun were to come up in the north instead of the east and go down in the south instead of the west?

The answer, of course is, no. This is all in God's hands. Day and night appear without fail. The light appears at the appointed place; then evening falls and no man can stop it or slow it down. We take these things for granted, but who established these laws? We have to get back to the first cause which is God Himself.

Men can forecast the time of the sunrise and sunset and tell us when there is going to be an eclipse of the sun or the moon. But men are not able to alter such times, not by one iota. God gave the command at the beginning and set these laws in motion and no one but He can alter them. We have some illustrations in the Scriptures of times when

God did alter His laws in respect to night and day. The 10th chapter of Joshua records how Joshua under obedience to God commanded the sun to stand still and it obeyed. The day was lengthened. How this was done we have no way of knowing. Only God could change these laws in the universe and yet not upset the universe. According to the language of that chapter in Joshua, the sun and the moon stood still for the space of about a day giving Joshua just that much more light to fight a crucial battle.

In the days of Hezekiah God set the sun back ten degrees, something that only He could do. Isaiah tells us that God said, "I form the light, and create darkness" (45:7).

Light reveals things whereas darkness hides them. This is what we learn in Ephesians 5:13 when this principle is applied in the moral realm: "But all things that are reproved are made manifest by the light: for whatsoever doth make manifest is light."

Men walk in spiritual darkness and blindness, refusing to acknowledge God's power around them. They refuse to come to the light that He has provided for them lest their deeds should be reproved. Nevertheless, this very reluctance on their part condemns them, for John 3:19-21 says, "And this is the condemnation, that light is come into the world, and men loved darkness rather than light, because their deeds were evil. For every one that doeth evil hateth the light, neither cometh to the light, lest his deeds should be reproved. But he that doeth truth cometh to the light, that his deeds may be made manifest, that they are wrought in God." Evil hides in the darkness but the light exposes it and at the same time manifests the things of God.

The coming Day of the Lord will be exactly of the same nature. It will reveal the evil of the night of the Tribulation. God who is the Creator of light will shake the wickedness out of the night. We are told that the new heavens and the new earth will have nothing to defile them. There will be no night there. Hallelujah!

Light speaks of righteousness. Shall Job accuse Him of wrong who is all-righteous, who sees all things, and who knows the secrets of all hearts? Job himself was in a spiritual form of darkness but God was going to deliver him in the proper time.

Gates of Death and Breadth of the Earth

God continued His questioning of Job by asking, "Have you explored the springs of the sea? Or have you walked in the recesses of the deep? Have the gates of death been revealed to you? Or have you seen the doors of deep darkness? Have you comprehended the breadth of the earth? Tell it, if you know it all" (vv. 16-18). These are very penetrating questions and though much is being done in the exploration of the seas today, is there much that modern man could answer with regard to these things?

Death is common to all of us and to every society of men but there are mysteries in it that only God can fathom.

Apparently more than merely measuring the breadth of the earth is in mind here. Job had said of God in chapter 28:24: "For he looks to the ends of the earth, and sees everything under the heavens." This no man or combination of men can do. Job had himself admitted this, and now God brings it before him again.

God uses irony here but not with the purpose of crushing Job but to bring him to his senses.

In verse 19 God asks, "Where is the way where light dwells? And as for darkness, where is its abode, That ye may conduct it to its home, and may know the paths to its house?" The phrase "way of light" is a statement that we might say is scientifically correct. The Amplified has an interesting note on this which reads: "How, except by divine inspiration, could Job have known that light does not dwell in a *place* but a *way*? For light, as modern man has discovered, involves motion, wave motion and travelling 186,000 miles a second it can only dwell in a *way*.

We learn from Genesis 1 that light was created before the light-giving bodies of the heavens were made visible. The sun is not *the* source of light, but is *a* source of light. The Lord uses some further irony on Job when He says, "You must know, since you were born then? Or because you are so extremely old!" (vv. 20,21). This was said not to belittle Job but to bring him to the place where he would recognize his limitations and insufficiencies. If he could not discern the path of light, how could he comprehend the way that God, who is the Light, wants to lead all who are redeemed?

Snow and Hail

More of the natural elements around us are mentioned in verse 22: "Have you entered the treasuries of the snow, or have you seen the treasuries of the hail, Which I have reserved for the time of trouble, for the day of battle and war?" These are remarkable statements. They indicate God's wisdom and power, His benevolences and also His judgments. The snow provides protection and moisture whereas the hail almost without exception is destructive. It brings judgment.

We read in Isaiah 28:17: "Judgment also will I lay to the line, and righteousness to the plummet: and the hail shall sweep away the refuge of lies, and the waters shall overflow the hiding place." Very clearly God is indicating here that He has reserved hail for judgment.

In the 10th chapter of Joshua to which we have previously referred, Joshua went out against the five kings of the Canaanites and God sent hail to help His servants overcome their enemies.

In the last book in the Bible we read: "And there fell upon men a great hail out of heaven, every stone about the weight of a talent: and men blasphemed God" (Rev. 16:21).

A scientist would say that snow is produced by the action of cold upon vapor, turning its molecules into crystals of lovely and varied forms. But we must remember these forms are planned. They are not accidental. Whose laws are fulfilled by these tiny crystals? Who designs their intricate patterns? Only an Infinite Mind could do this. This is the work of our God!

Then the Bible speaks of the whiteness of snow as a symbol of the covering of sin. "Come now, and let us reason together, saith the Lord: though your sins be as scarlet, they shall be white as snow" (Isa. 1:18).

God asked Job if he knew the resources for good or resources for war and judgment that God has. Could he tell where they come from? Did Job understand the resources of God for his needs when he ran into times of trouble? God appeared to Job as the great I AM, indicating to him: "Whatever you need, Job, that is what I am for you."

Job's battle was too big for him. He did not know the resources of strength that God had for him in the midst of the darkness he was seeking to have dispelled. But then, if Job had not known this time of darkness, we would possibly have never learned, at least not through Job's experience, how God removed that darkness.

We know from the Word that we can do all things through Christ who strengthens us (Phil. 4:13). We are also told that we are to be strong in the Lord and in the power of His might, because we wrestle not against flesh and blood but against principalities and powers, against the rulers of the darkness of this world, against spiritual wickedness in heavenly places (Eph. 6:10-12). God has all the resources we need.

The more we see of God the less we will think of ourselves. Many times I have gone back to this passage in Job to encourage my faith in the greatness of God. To me this has been one of the most beneficial studies I have undertaken. In coming to see something of the greatness of God I have also seen how deeply concerned He is with every detail of my life and the lives of all His people.

Job whose knowledge when compared with other men seems to be outstanding, is brought to the place where he realizes that according to God's standards He knows very little. Still Job knew some things that scientists today are just finding out.

The Lord asked Job if he knew how light is distributed. His question was: "By what is the light distributed, or the east wind spread over the earth?" (v. 24).

Light to the naked eye is usually seen as white but when put through a prism, it is broken up into its various colors. Some of this is evident in the rainbow and in the sunsets. We now know that certain substances reflect a certain light ray which in turn is produced by certain rapid vibrations. But we find there is more to light than this. For example, the X ray is a form of light that has power to penetrate certain substances. By use of the X ray man can see what cannot be seen by the naked eye alone. Then there are ultraviolet rays and a so-called red ray which is a heat ray.

Modern science has much to tell us here that fills us with wonder, but what shall we worship as a result, science or God?

White light, we are told, is composed of three main rays, blue, green and red. These in combinations throughout the spectrum form other related colors.

The Bible uses the word "light" to describe God. First John tells us that God is light. As we have seen, pure light is white. Yet that pure light is composed of three basic colors. This is possibly as close an illustration of the Trinity as we will find. Each color has its own separate position and usefulness, yet the three together compose what we call "light." God is One in essence, but the Godhead is composed of three separate Persons—Father, Son, and Holy Spirit.

Science tells us there are three kinds of light rays. There is the ray that enables us to see. There is a ray which gives out heat. Then there is a third ray that is the chemical or radiant ray or a life-giving ray. These are interrelated and complement each other.

How wonderful all of this is. First there is light, but light without heat would destroy creation. If the light ray and the heat ray are combined they also would make havoc of creation. But put all three together, adding the radiant or so-called healing ray, and we have light which makes life possible. This again presents a good illustration of the Trinity, all of whom have separate responsibilities in salvation and all of whose works are needed in providing a complete salvation for the believer.

The Lord turned to another part of His creation when He asked Job, "Who has prepared gullies [in the sky] for the torrents of rain, or a path for the thunderbolt" (v. 25). Only an all-wise God would know how to distribute the rains over the earth. In spite of all of man's talk about controlling the weather this is still something that is in God's hands. Would we, like Job, question the wisdom of One who shows His infinite power from day to day in this realm?

Furthermore, since God directs the forces that have to do with the rain and the rivers that play such a large part in providing man's food, can we not trust Him to direct our lives and supply our needs? This was what Job needed to learn, and the truth was undoubtedly beginning to bear fruit in his life.

The Heavenly Bodies and Clouds and Rain

The Lord then turned Job's attention to the stars, the heavenly bodies, bringing before Job's mind something of the magnitude of the visible universe. We are told that the constellations turn around some unknown center. They appear to our eye as though they barely move, if they

seem to move at all, but the fact is they travel with in-
conceivable swiftness. The stars move in orbits established
by God and do whatever He desires. Their numbers are
so great that we cannot compute the total, but God can
and even has named each one.

This is the testimony of Isaiah 40:26: "Lift up your
eyes on high, and behold who hath created these things,
that bringeth out their hosts by number: he calls them
all by names by the greatness of his might, for that he
is strong in power; not one faileth." This is our God. This
is the God whom Job dared to accuse of mistreating him.
So God simply asked him if he could loose or lead forth
the stars in their courses. He asked him if he could establish the ordinances of heaven. He asked him if he could
lift up his voice to the clouds so that he might be supplied
with plenty of water. He also asked him if he could send
the lightning when and where he pleased. These are enough
to overwhelm any man who recognizes his limitations. No
one but the sovereign Lord of heaven and earth could so
easily summarize these matters and show that all the forces
of nature are at His absolute command.

A man piloting a large plane watches his many instruments and by manipulation of levers and buttons and
switches guides the huge vehicle. This to me has always
been a matter for wonder. But the God of the universe
controls every minute detail of the universe including
all that is on the earth. Then why question His ability to
do what needs to be done for us? And why resist or resent what He does for us?

No wonder the Psalmist cried, "When I consider thy
heavens, the work of thy fingers, the moon and the stars
which thou hast ordained; What is man, that thou art mindful of him? and the son of man that thou visitest him?"

Then in the 104th Psalm we read: "Who coverest thyself
with light as with a garment: who stretchest out the heavens
like a curtain: Who layeth the beams of his chambers in

the waters: who maketh the clouds his chariot: who walketh upon the wings of the wind . . . Who laid the foundations of the earth, that it should not be removed for ever.
Thou coveredst it with the deep as with a garment: the
waters stood above the mountains. At thy rebuke they
fled; at the voice of thy thunder they hasted away. . . . Thou
hast set a bound that they may not pass over; that they
turn not again to cover the earth.

"He sendeth the springs into the valleys, which run
among the hills. They give drink to every beast of the
field: the wild asses quench their thirst. . . . He causeth
the grass to grow for the cattle, and herb for the service
of man: that he may bring forth food out of the earth. . . .
The trees of the Lord are full of sap; the cedars of Lebanon,
which he hath planted. . . . He appointed the moon for
seasons: the sun knoweth his going down. Thou makest
darkness, and it is night: wherein all the beasts of the forest
do creep forth."

This is an excellent commentary on this portion of
Job now under consideration. Without the power, planning
and constant supervision of God these things would not
be possible. But because He is who He is, life goes on and
God's people can with confidence look to the future knowing He is taking care of them.

If we live by Romans 8:28 which states that we know
that all things work together for good to them that love
the Lord, we will have a basis for deep-seated contentment
and peace that nothing else could bring. We may not have
happiness in the sense that the world uses that word, but
we will have joy in the Bible sense.

CHAPTER THIRTEEN

GOD'S CARE OF HIS CREATION

In His next approach to Job, the Lord changes the subject matter of His discourse though He stays with the general thought of creation. He changes from His supervision of the stars in the heavens and the elements that have to do with life on earth to His care over the creatures of His creation. God wanted Job to become fully aware that the God who cared for every creature on the earth would most certainly make adequate provision for man whom He had created in His own image. Since God is so thoughtful for animal life on the earth, how much more will His care be for one whom He loves! He sent the Saviour to die for us and is preparing heaven for all of us who trust in Christ.

Do we think that God is going to let us endure the storms of life and care nothing for us? God has filled the earth with living creatures who are absolutely dependent upon Him for life and for the sustenance of life. His goodness and providence are illustrated all around us. How foolish we are to mistrust Him.

In the passage before us the Lord raises seven distinct questions with reference to His care concerning His creatures. He opens the list and closes it by mentioning animals and birds of prey. This may amaze us, for we are sometimes inclined to think of these creatures as either worthless or actually injurious. Nevertheless, we read here that He takes care of them with unerring wisdom. Do we imagine for a moment that He would be less concerned about an individual who had placed trust in Him?

The Lion and the Raven

The Lord says according to 38:39-41: "Can you [Job] hunt the prey for the lion? Or satisfy the appetite of the young lions, When they couch in their dens, or lie in wait in their hiding place? Who provides for the raven its prey, when its young ones cry to God and wander about for lack of food?" What would happen if man had to provide food for the creatures for just one day? This is exactly what the Lord is asking Job. It is not a question of one lion or one raven but all such creatures together.

The Psalmist commented on this in various places, for to him it was a mark of God's wisdom and power that all the lower creation waited upon God for their food and He provided them with it in due season. God opened His hand and they were filled with His provision (Ps. 104).

We cannot escape the fact that God created these animals that prey on others. God makes provision for them as they need it. The instincts of such animals are provided by God, even though men may speak of "mother nature" in place of God.

Before sin came into the world all these creatures were subject to man. Now some of them, especially the flesh-eaters, are man's enemies. Nevertheless, God takes care of them. He has a place in His program for them just as He has a place for Satan at the present time. The Evil One was allowed to test Job up to a certain point until God's desired work had been done in His child's heart.

Our Saviour referred to God's care of creation when He said, "Consider the ravens: for they neither sow nor reap; which neither have storehouse nor barn. . . . God feedeth them: how much more are ye better than the fowls?" (Luke 12:24).

Animals in the High Mountains

In the 39th chapter of Job God speaks of animals that inhabit some of the almost inaccessible places such as the rugged mountain areas of the earth. The Lord asked: "Do you know the time when the wild goats of the rock bring forth [their young]? Or observe when the hinds are giving birth? [Do you attend to all this, Job?] (v. 1). In the 4th verse the statement is made: "Their young ones become strong, they grow up in the open field; they go forth, and return not to them." The Lord has different ways of taking care of different animals. In the case of these just mentioned the young spend only a short time with their parents and then they go out on their own. Who takes care of them? God does.

If God so takes care of the animals that climb rocks, shall He not watch the steps of His timid people who must climb over the rugged rocks of adversity? Job could hardly miss the point of this question. The Lord also speaks of the moment of birth and of death. This is something that individuals do not know but God does since He knows all things.

Job had cried out for deliverance and he had also cried out for death. But only God knew when the travail of Job's soul had reached the place where God's purposes were accomplished in him. It was then that the trials would be lifted.

Let us learn to leave our cares to the wisdom of God. He knows how much and how far to go in every case. There are many different types of trials people pass through. I wonder sometimes how some individuals can stand up under the tests they face. But God gives His own people marvelous grace for these things.

The Wild Donkey

In verses 5 through 7 the Lord asks two more questions. These verses read: "Who has sent out the wild donkey, giving him his freedom and his unconquerable love of liberty? Or who has loosed the bands of the swift donkey [by which his tame brother is bound—he, the shy, the swift-footed and the untamable], Whose home I have made the wilderness, and the salt land his dwelling place? He scorns the tumult of the city, and hears not the shoutings of the taskmaster." The wild donkey the Lord speaks of is completely different in habits and disposition from the donkeys my wife and I saw by the thousands in the various lands of the East. Yet these, too, like all of God's creatures are, in the final analysis, dependent upon Him for life and food. The wild donkey is one that cannot be tamed. It cannot be used by man, and for that reason many persons would consider it useless. Yet God looks after this creature and has a place in His plans for it.

The Wild Ox

Concerning the wild ox God asked Job: "Will the wild ox be willing to serve you, or remain beside your manger? Can you bind the wild ox with harness to the plow in the furrow? Or will he harrow the furrows for you? Will you trust him, because his strength is great, or to him will you leave your labor? Will you depend upon him to bring home your seed and gather the grain of your threshing floor? [Who, Job, was the author of this strange variance in disposition of animals so alike in appearance? Was it you?]" (vv. 9-12).

The tame ox was once widely used for hauling loads and cultivating the soil in this country. It is still one of the main sources of power in many parts of the East today. But that is the tame ox. What the Lord is speaking of here is the one that man cannot tame. It is an animal that can neither be trusted nor controlled. Yet God makes provision for it.

The Ostrich

The next creature dealt with is the ostrich. This is an unusual bird for it seems to be devoid of any maternal instincts. It has no care for its young at all. The female leaves her eggs on the ground to be warmed in the dust. Apparently she forgets that a foot may crush them or a wild animal trample on them. "She is hardened against her young ones, as though they were not hers; her labor is in vain because she has no sense of danger [for her unborn brood]. For God has deprived her of wisdom, neither has He imparted to her understanding. Yet when she lifts up herself in flight, [so swift is she] that she can laugh to scorn the horse and his rider" (vv. 16-18).

Here is a creature that is unlike most of the others because it does not care for its young. It does not have the mother instinct that makes it guard the eggs, then provide for the young once they are hatched. But here again, God provides for the little brood. The very way the eggs are hidden protects them from enemies. Then, we are told, much of the egg serves as food for the newly hatched bird. This is not chance but providence. Here again is proof of the wisdom of God in caring for His creatures and further assurance of His caring for His children.

The War Horse

The next animal spoken of is the war horse. The words are: "Have you given the horse his might? Have you clothed his neck with quivering, and a shaking mane? Was it you, Job, who made him to leap like a locust? The majesty of his (snorting) nostrils is terrible. He paws in the valley, and exults in his strength; he goes out to meet the weapons (of armed men). He mocks at fear, and is not dismayed or terrified; neither does he turn back [in battle] from the sword. The quiver rattles upon him, as do the glittering spear and the lance [of his rider]. He seems in running to devour the ground with fierceness and rage; neither can he stand still at the sound of the war trumpet. As often as the trumpet sounds he says, Ha, ha! And he smells the battle from afar, the thunder of the captains, and the shouting" (vv. 19-25).

Perhaps few reading this have seen such an animal. We have all undoubtedly seen the horse that is common to the peaceful pursuits of men, but the subject here is the war horse. This is no gentle animal though it often has grace and beauty combined with strength and fearlessness. The noise of battle is music to this creature's ears. But who created this creature? Who made him different from the other horses and who made provision for him?

The Lord warned the nation of Israel against placing confidence in the strength of a horse. His ancient people were to find their defence in Him and not in such fierce and rugged creatures. He forbade the Israelites to multiply horses for war. Nevertheless, God made provision for the preservation of these dangerous animals also.

The Hawk and the Eagle

The hawk and the eagle are both birds of prey. The Lord asks concerning them: "Is it by your wisdom [Job] that the hawk soars and stretches her wings toward the south [as winter approaches]? Does the eagle mount up at your command, and make his nest on a high inaccessible place? On the cliff he dwells and remains securely, upon the point of the rock and the stronghold. From there he spies out the prey, and his eyes see it afar off. His young ones suck up blood, and where the slain are, there is he" (vv. 26-30). In this portion the Lord speaks of the migratory habits of birds and the custom of the eagle to build its nest in the high inaccessible mountains or rocks and his remarkable ability to see his prey from a long distance away. Who provided them with these instincts and powers? These are not accidental matters. Again God is emphasizing the fact that He created these birds for a reason.

Perhaps you have seen, as I have, an eagle's nest on some high rocky crag. Or you may have seen him soaring into the sky, then suddenly plummeting to the earth to catch his prey. He is doing this because he was made by God to do it.

We read in the Book of the Revelation that after the Battle of Armageddon God will call the birds of the air together to feast on the slain. Birds of prey have a very definite place in the plans and purposes of God.

The Lord brought these matters down to a level Job could fully comprehend. These various creatures are provided for by the hand of the Creator. The point is that since He does this for the birds and animals, how much more is He concerned for His suffering saint. We cannot but utter Paul's doxology which he gave when he pondered God's dealing with Israel: "O the depth of the riches both of the wisdom and knowledge of God! how unsearchable are his judgments, and his ways past finding out!" (Rom. 11:33).

How Was Job Affected?

Have we come to fully realize that there is absolutely no good thing in us? Our fallen natures are corrupt. They cannot be reformed, they can do nothing good. On the other hand, God can do no evil. So our natural selves and God stand at opposite poles. The one is evil and the other absolutely righteous.

This may be hard for us to admit, but it was just as hard for Job. The Lord said to him: "Shall he who would find fault with the Almighty contend with Him? He who reproves and disputes with God, let him answer Me." Job replied, "Behold I am of small account and vile! What shall I answer You? I lay my hand upon my mouth. I have spoken once, but I will not reply again; indeed, twice [have I answered], but I will proceed no further" (Job 40:4,5). This is Job's response at the end of this part of God's dealing with him. The patriarch began to see that he had spoken hastily. Someone has said in describing this scene: "He (God) has taken as it were the clay of creation and put it upon the eyes of the poor sufferer who had been blinded by his own griefs and to all the power and the wisdom and goodness of God." Will Job now go and in the words of the New Testament "wash in the pool of Siloam"? Is Job ready to bow in full submission before his Creator?

Job must have been unaware of the workings of his fallen nature. Many of us are like him. We do not realize how subtle that evil nature is. Unless we know through the Word the habits and cunning of our carnal nature, we are going to be trapped as Job was trapped. The new birth does not change "the old man." The new birth is the entrance of Christ into our life to control it, but that does not change or transform the old nature in any way. It cannot be tamed or trained. It is of no use to God and it is a danger to us. It is no wonder God has told us that we must not yield our members as instruments of unrighteousness unto sin (another name for the fallen nature), but we are to yield ourselves to God as those who are alive from the dead and our members instruments of righteousness unto God.

Job had contended with God. He had argued against God's dealing with him which, of course, was the root of his problem. He, the creature, had sat in judgment upon

God the Creator. He had gone so far as to accuse God of doing the wrong thing.

Now God had drawn near and made His presence known and felt. From nature He had drawn very obvious lessons so that Job could not fail to catch the moral principles involved. No wonder Job replied that he was vile.

He was not the only one who has come face to face with himself and been humbled. There was a time when Ezra, having seen how his own people were disobeying God, said, "O my God, I am ashamed and blush to lift up my face to thee, my God: for our iniquities are increased over our head, and our trespass is grown up unto the heavens" (Ezra 9:6).

What could Job really answer God after this revelation of God's care of His creatures? Job felt in his own heart how contemptible he had been in speaking as he did of the Lord. He had thought the Lord cruel and unjust. In reality God had worked His own purpose of love in Job's heart. Job decided all he could do was put his hand on his mouth, say nothing more, and just listen to God.

How are we when we pass through times of suffering? Do we wonder after the testing has endured a long time if God really cares? We seek for sympathy and God in His grace is ready and willing to give it, but above all we must remember that God has permitted this testing and has a purpose in it. God is both sovereign and righteous, so in His sovereignty He always does what is right.

Remember again Jeremiah who, when passing through a time of very severe trials, said, "For the Lord will not cast off for ever: But though he cause grief, yet will he have compassion according to the multitude of his mercies. For he doth not afflict willingly [that means afflict with pleasure] nor grieve the children of men" (Lam. 3:31-33).

If we do wrong we suffer for the wrong done. On the other hand, much suffering in the life of a believer is disciplinary and not punitive. And through such suffering

God molds us into the image of His Son (Rom. 8:28,29). This, all unknown to Job, was actually taking place in his life.

We must not forget that Job was an outstanding man and an unusual believer. He expressed a wonderful faith in the midst of his sufferings on several occasions. It is true that in places he faltered. He did not have the light we have that tells us of the conflict between the old nature and the Holy Spirit. Nor did he know that victory comes when we let the Holy Spirit control us.

Job's Response to His First Trials

Remember how Job responded after the first attack of Satan? The patriarch had lost everything by way of possessions and children. When word was brought to him he rose to his feet, rent his clothes, shaved his head, then fell down upon the ground "and worshipped." Do we realize the strength of faith in this man who in the face of such bitter loss would worship and not complain?

In his worship he said, "Naked came I out of my mother's womb, and naked shall I return thither: the Lord gave, and the Lord hath taken away; blessed be the name of the Lord. In all this Job sinned not, nor charged God foolishly" (Job 1:21,22, KJV).

The next time we have a record of Job speaking was right after Satan had smitten him with a terrible disease. Job's wife had been left to him. Apparently no harm had come to her, but Satan used her for his own purposes at the time of Job's illness. She asked her husband why he did not curse God and die. It was, in effect, a suggestion that he take his own life. But the patriarch answered her, "Thou speakest as one of the foolish women speaketh. What? Shall we receive good at the hand of God, and shall we not receive evil? In all this did not Job sin with his lips" (2:10, KJV).

Later on when Job's friends accused him of having

committed sins that he was seeking to hide he stated: "Though he slay me, yet will I trust in him: but I will maintain mine own ways before him. He also shall be my salvation: for an hypocrite shall not come before him" (13:15,16, KJV).

When Job's friends had made a second round of accusations against him he expressed his faith in these words: "For I know that my redeemer liveth, and that he shall stand at the latter day upon the earth: And though after my skin worms destroy this body, yet in my flesh shall I see God: Whom I shall see for myself, and mine eyes shall behold, and not another; though my reins be consumed within me" (19:25-27, KJV).

After a long futile search for God, though God was not far away, Job comforted himself with this assuring truth: "But he knoweth the way that I take: when he hath tried me, I shall come forth as gold" (23:10, KJV).

In his concluding answer to his friends, Job made this glorious statement: "And unto man he said, Behold, the fear of the Lord, that is wisdom; and to depart from evil is understanding" (28:28, KJV). Thus we see that during Job's crying out in the night time of his afflictions he stated many beautiful and noble thoughts.

A Better Response

But none of these are to be compared to these few words by which he indicated he was beginning to see the error of his thoughts about God. Even the beginning of such a confession on his part was music in the ears of God. There was still more to be learned, but a good beginning had been made. The Spirit of God would carry it on through to completion. Job was no longer justifying himself. He had come to see himself as unworthy, and he loathed himself.

When David acknowledged the depths of his sin God

was able to deal with him to bring him back to fellowship and put him on the road of usefulness again. The same was true with Job. He came to see God in a new way and he saw himself in a new way also. He saw how small he was in comparison to the universe and God's infinite care of everything.

Job had yet to see that he was unwise in his accusation. He said that he was vile and of small account. But he also had to realize that so far as his fallen nature was concerned he was depraved and not capable of any good. And he must see that God was entirely righteous and not capable of any evil. God could not do wrong nor use poor judgment. It was impossible for Him to make a mistake. These were some of the adjustments in his thinking that Job had to come to.

He was made silent as he saw the majesty, power and wisdom of God. He was convinced that such a Being whose perfections were displayed before him cannot be arbitrary and unjust in His dealings with man.

CHAPTER FOURTEEN

GOD'S FINAL LESSON FOR JOB

God's purpose in this final lesson to Job is to deepen the impressions already made upon him. The Lord has no intentions of leaving His servant with lessons only half learned. So God plowed more deeply into Job's heart until the hidden depths of pride and self were reached and judged. This is why God took up pride which is so common to the creatures of God and showed how it operates even among the animals.

In His previous address to Job the Lord dealt largely with His providential care for His creatures. In this final appeal He speaks of His authority over creatures that defy man's control. There is a type of pride in them which combined with their immense strength and resistlessness provides a very powerful lesson for God's servant. The question God asks is, "Can you control them, Job?" Has Job not placed himself morally in the company of these animals that resist man inasmuch as he, Job, has lifted up himself against God?

The patriarch needed the experience of the Psalmist who was distressed and distraught over the prosperity of the wicked. It was a subject too painful for this man of God until he went into the sanctuary and saw what God had to reveal concerning the latter end of these wicked men. Then the Psalmist said, "Thus my heart was grieved, and I was pricked in my reins. So foolish was I, and ignorant: I was as a beast before thee" (Ps. 73:21,22).

It was to bring him to this place that God called upon Job to consider how far he would get in handling the powerful and stubborn creatures in God's creation. We read: "Then the Lord answered Job out of the whirlwind, saying, Gird up your loins now like a man; I will demand of you, and you answer Me. Will you also annul—set aside and render void—My judgment? Will you condemn Me [your God] that you may appear righteous and justified?" (vv. 40:6-8). The Lord touched on the heart of Job's problem when He asked him if he would condemn His God so that he, Job, might appear righteous and justified.

Have we unwittingly fallen into the same sin? In our ignorance and because of our heartaches and possible mistreatments by others, have we accused God of not treating us fairly? This was Job's experience but it means little to us unless we examine our own lives in the light of it.

Job could no longer justify himself after God's dealing with him. So he confessed he was of small account. He felt humbled and contemptible and mean before God. He confessed that he ought not to have spoken as he did, and he also said that he would proceed no further in this kind of folly. But more was needed to bring Job to true repentance. He had been silenced so far as self-justification is concerned when he saw the greatness of God. He still needed to be reminded that all the good things he had done in the past were not the result of his having a better-than-average human nature but were the result of God's work in him.

Job had to see that he was totally helpless to perform the righteousness of God apart from the life of God. The principle involved here is enunciated in Luke 9:23 where our Lord said, "If any man will come after me, let him deny himself [see himself as helpless], and take up his cross daily [the place of death toward self], and follow me." This is the Christian life in a nutshell just as John 3:16 is the gospel in a nutshell.

Job Invited to Take the Throne

God continued His dealing with Job by asking: "Have you an arm like God? Or can you thunder with a voice like His?" (v. 9). Was Job's arm of flesh as powerful as the omnipotent power of God? Could Job thunder with his voice and shake the nations? The answer is obvious.

The Lord continued: "[Since you question the manner of the Almighty's rule] deck yourself now with the excellency and dignity [of the supreme Ruler, and yourself undertake the government of the world, if you are so wise], and array yourself with honor and majesty" (v. 10). The folly of Job's statements became increasingly evident. It would be utterly impossible for him to take the government of the world and to array himself in honor and majesty in such a way that the world would honor him. Job could not administer the affairs of God better than He could. Could we?

God challenged Job to pour out his anger so as to humble the proud man and bring him low. The Lord said, "Look on every one who is proud, and bring him low, and tread down the wicked where they stand [if you are so able, Job]. Bury and hide them all in the dust together, and shut them up [in the prison house of death]" (vv. 12,13). This is irony but it is divine irony. It is not designed to crush Job but to humble him.

Something of the terrible majesty of God in judgment is pictured for us in the Book of the Revelation. We read that with the opening of the sixth seal "there was a great earthquake; and the sun became black as sackcloth of hair, and the moon became as blood; And the stars of heaven fell unto the earth, even as a fig tree casteth her untimely figs, when she is shaken of a mighty wind. And the heaven departed as a scroll when it is rolled together; and every

mountain and island were moved out of their places. And
the kings of the earth, and the great men, and the rich men,
and the chief captains, and the mighty men, and every bondman, and every free man, hid themselves in the dens and
in the rocks of the mountains; And said to the mountains
and rocks, Fall on us, and hide us from the face of him
that sitteth on the throne, and from the wrath of the Lamb:
For the great day of his wrath is come; and who shall be
able to stand?" (6:12-17).

So God is in effect asking Job if he could make the
nations shake as God will one day make them fear. Would
Job be able to make the world itself shake so that mountains disappear? Could a mere man black out the sun
and the moon and so frighten the rulers of the world that
they would hide themselves in caves and acknowledge that
God is really God?

Another verse to consider in this line of truth is Genesis
12:3 where the Lord said to Abraham: "And I will bless them
that bless thee, and curse him that curseth thee: and in thee
shall all the families of the earth be blessed." So Job might
well have been asked if he could bless the nations that bless
Israel and curse and judge the nations that cursed Israel.
Anyone who would seek to pass judgment on the ways of
God with men would have to have such powers before he
would have the right to speak.

So it was that God said to Job: "[If you can do all this,
Job, proving yourself of divine might] then will I, God,
praise you also and acknowledge that your own right hand
can save you" (v. 14). These things of which God had
spoken are possible only to an omnipotent God. And only
He has the right to judge men and shut them up in the
prison house of death. Job as a mere man could do none
of these things. Job had not shown himself wise so that
God might seek Him for advice.

Job had not been able to control his own heart. Not
only had he not brought that under control, but he had not

humbled his friends who falsely accused him. How far short was he, then, of bringing the whole earth into submission. Job could not even bring himself back to where he had once been spiritually.

If Job had been so great why did he not stop the thieves that drove off his possessions? Why did he not halt the terrible tornado and put out the fire that took the last of what he had? Why was he sitting on an ash heap in great pain of body if he were in control of all things?

These were questions Job had to face in order to see his own nothingness in the presence of the majesty and boundless good of Almighty God. God was slowly bringing His servant to a place of emptiness so that He could fill him with future blessing.

The Hippopotamus

God had one more lesson for Job. In this particular lesson He spoke about two of the most formidable creatures He had created. To see their characteristics is to be reminded of two factors in the life of a child of God: one, the old nature, and the other, the self-will of man.

The first animal mentioned is the behemoth or the hippopotamus. It is becoming known to many of us through some of the larger zoos. After reading God's description of this animal we will have a great deal of respect for it.

God said of it: "Behold now behemoth (the hippopotamus), which I created as I did you; he eats grass as an ox. See now, his strength is in his loins, and his power is in the sinews of his belly. He moves his tail like a cedar tree; the tendons of his thighs are twisted together [like a rope]. His bones are as tubes of bronze; his limbs and ribs are like bars of iron. The hippopotamus is the first [in magnitude and power] of the works of God in animal life; only He who made him provides him with his sword-like tusks, and God Who made him, alone can bring near His sword [to master him]. Surely the mountains bring him forth food, where all the wild animals play. He lies under the lotus trees, in the covert of the reeds and in the marsh. The lotus trees cover him with their shade; the willows of the brook compass him about. Behold, if a river is violent and overflows, he does not tremble; he is confident though a Jordan River swells and rushes against his mouth. Can any take him when he is on the watch, or pierce through his nose with a snare?" (40:15-24).

In the 19th verse God calls him the chief or first in magnitude and power of all His animal creation. Every portion of the anatomy of this creature speaks of tremendous strength. Yet he eats grass like an ox. Other animals feed in the same field as he does. He seems harmless and is harmless unless aroused. That may be the reason other animals are not afraid of him. But one dare not get in his way, or eat what he wants to eat. He thinks only of himself and his anger is easily aroused.

He rests when and where he wants to. He is not afraid of anyone or anything. Even if the river is raging in flood, it does not disturb him. He is perfectly safe, for he is at home in the water as well as on the land. He cannot be caught in a trap or held with cords or even controlled with rings through his nostrils. In other words, he is untamable and uncontrollable. God made him so.

Furthermore, he cannot be harnessed for work. Men cannot make him pull a plow like they do an ox.

In our travels we saw many a person plowing his field with an ox, or a donkey, or a water buffalo or even a camel. But nowhere did I see anyone who had a hippopotamus hitched to a plow or a cultivator. Yet he is such a strong animal he might have been made to pull half a dozen plows —if he could just be tamed.

This creature reminds us of the old fallen nature in each of us. This is what God taught Job here, showing him what the old nature is like. But this was not written for the patriarch's sake alone. It was written for our learning also. I have learned from my study of the Scripture not to take this truth concerning the old nature in a light manner. If we are to understand ourselves and the victory God has for us in overcoming sin in our lives, we must recognize that so far as man is concerned the Adamic nature is untamable and uncontrollable. It renders no good service; in fact it is an enemy. Only the Lord, the Creator, can control it.

So far as Job was concerned his old nature had not been brought under control but had been allowed to dominate his thinking and reaction during part of his testing. But God knew how to provide victory for him, and it was the Lord who eventually brought Job's fallen nature under perfect control. Job, however, had to see these matters for himself. He had to realize that his old nature needed to be brought under the control of God.

As the mighty hippopotamus was not frightened when the floods surrounded him, so Job needed to learn that all of life's events are in God's hands. The floods of adversity could not overwhelm him. God would see him through. He could not sink since he was in the hands of God. We, too, who have trusted in Christ are in the hands of God. The Lord Jesus has promised that no man shall pluck His own out of His hands. He has promised to take us by the hand and lead us in paths of righteousness and peace.

This is the testimony of the Psalmist who said: "For this shall every one that is godly pray unto thee in a time when thou mayest be found: surely in the floods of great waters they shall not come nigh unto him" (32:6).

That is a wonderful verse for us, and here is another: "When thou passest through the waters, I will be with thee; and through the rivers, they shall not overflow thee: when thou walkest through the fire, thou shalt not be burned; neither shall the flame kindle upon thee" (Isa. 43:2).

Turn to the New Testament to the 8th chapter of Romans and see some more of the wonderful provision God has made for us: "What shall we then say to these things? If God be for us, who can be against us? He that spared not his own Son, but delivered him up for us all, how shall he not with him also freely give us all things? Who shall lay anything to the charge of God's elect? It is God that justifieth. Who is he that condemneth? It is Christ that died, yea rather, that is risen again, who is even at the right hand of God, who also maketh intercession for us" (vv. 31-34).

These are only some of the marvelous promises of God. Why not trust Him? If God can tame the mighty hippopotamus which humanly speaking is untamable; if He has perfect control of it and takes care of it and preserves it, cannot He be trusted to give us the victory over the old nature and take care of us as His children? He loves us dearly, so we can trust Him to do this and much more!

This great beast lives only for itself. If left alone, it probably will not bother any one. But stir it up and it kicks up a great deal of trouble. That is exactly what we must learn about the old nature. Leave it alone, cater to it, give it anything it wants and there will be little or no battle in our hearts over it. But if we say, no, to our fallen nature we can look for plenty of trouble. Had not Job's old nature responded just like the hippopotamus that had been stirred up suddenly?

When Job was first tried, he seemed to have control of his old nature or, as we might say, a measure of victory in his life. But when he was falsely accused, the old nature was aroused and Job was soon in deep trouble. It took him a long time to get out of it.

God dealt with him and showed him what he really was like apart from the grace of God. This is why God allows some things to come into our lives that may not always seem pleasant to us. It is to demonstrate to our own hearts and minds what we really are apart from the grace of God. Without the control of His Spirit we would be failures as believers.

One of the passages I treasure greatly is II Peter 1:3,4: "According as his divine power hath given unto us all things that pertain unto life and godliness, through the knowledge of him that hath called us to glory and virtue: Whereby are given unto us exceeding great and precious promises: that by these ye might be partakers of the divine nature, having escaped the corruption that is in the world through lust." This passage tells us very clearly that God has made us partakers of His nature. And since we are partakers of His nature we not only have His strength, power and might, to help us but He Himself takes charge of us and controls the old nature.

This is the teaching also of Galatians 5:16,17: "This I say then, Walk in the Spirit, and ye shall not fulfil the lust of the flesh. For the flesh lusteth against the Spirit, and the Spirit against the flesh: and these are contrary the one to the other: so that ye cannot do the things that ye would." So let us count on God to give us the victory over the fallen nature in us.

The Crocodile

In Job 41 God describes another powerful creature. It is called leviathan. In reality it was a large crocodile perhaps from the Nile River. The description of this animal is graphic and terrible. It is another creature which man cannot tame. God says of him: "Can you draw out leviathan [the crocodile] with a fishhook? Or press down his tongue with a cord? Can you put a rope into his nose? Or pierce his jaw through with a hook or a spike? Will he make many supplications to you [begging to be spared]? Will he speak soft words to you [to coax you to treat him kindly]? Will he make a covenant with you to take him for your servant forever? Will you play with the crocodile as with a bird? Or will you put him on leash for your maidens?" (vv. 1-5).

Just lay your hands on him once, God said, and you will not forget the battle you will have with him. You will not do such an ill-advised thing again. Then He added: "No one is so fierce and foolhardy that he dares to stir up the crocodile; who then is he who can stand before Me [the beast's Creator], or dares to contend with Me? Who has first given to Me, that I should repay him? Whatever is under the whole heavens is Mine. [Therefore, who can have a claim against God, God who made the unmastered crocodile?]" (41:10,11).

This creature of power and strength and evil reminds us of the self-will of self-willed men upon the earth. This is not something men can control by themselves, it takes divine power to effect this. Where self-will has gone unrestrained cruel conquerors have arisen. They are men like Nimrod, Nebuchadnezzar, the rulers of the Medes and the Persians, the Greeks, and the Romans. In our own day we remember such men as Hitler and Stalin. History has also witnessed the end of such men but there are always others to take their places. However, God has the last word. The unbeliever has no new nature, he has only an old nature. But whether it is the fallen nature found in either a believer or an unbeliever, its characteristic is as described in Romans 8:7: "Because the carnal mind [this is the old nature and the human will as controlled by the old nature] is enmity against God: for it is not subject to the law of God, neither indeed can be."

Just as the first beast had no fear of the floods, this second beast has a heart like stone and is indifferent to fear. Nevertheless, its heart is subject to God's influence and control. Job's heart was subject to the control of God also. He had argued that the Lord had taken away his rights, but God had pointed out that He was sovereign and whatever rights Job had were accorded him by the Lord. Actually, Job had no rights save only to submit himself to Almighty God.

The concluding words of this chapter as given in the Amplified are as follows: "[And now, Job, who are you, who dares not arouse the unmastered crocodile, yet who dares resist Me, the beast's Creator, to My face? Everything under the heavens is Mine; therefore who can have a claim against God?]" (v. 34).

CHAPTER FIFTEEN

VICTORY ACCOMPLISHED

The opening verses of Job 42 are the record of Job's confession to the Lord. That portion of the Book covers three main subjects, first, Job's evaluation of himself; second, his relationship to God; third, his relationship to his friends.

Job's Evaluation of Himself

Job saw God and this brought a new evaluation of himself. It was not until he saw God that he realized what kind of man he was apart from God's redeeming grace.

Job had begun to discover himself as the result of God's discourse in chapters 38 and 39. God opened up some wonderful things about the universe to Job and asked some very pointed questions which made Job realize some things about God and His power that he apparently had not grasped. The patriarch then acknowledged according to the 40th chapter that he was vile and had nothing more to say.

God could not be satisfied with this, though it was progress so far as Job's spiritual condition was concerned. There was still more truth for Job to become conscious of. His humbling of himself was a natural and inevitable result of having been ushered into the presence of God.

This does not mean that Job saw God face to face in a physical sense. It does mean that he had a new spiritual understanding of Him. This was not the result of dreams or hallucinations or visions. It was a new spiritual concept, something that could only be produced in the heart and mind by the Holy Spirit. Some people respond to this with despair, others again come out of despair and depression into joy and peace of heart and mind.

There is no part of God's creation as dear to Him as man. God created him for a very special purpose. And though man has reacted in rebellion against God, God still loves him. Job shows what man will do under certain circumstances. He had charged God foolishly. He even questioned the justice of God, the government of God, the wisdom of God, yet God was not discouraged with him. He knew the end from the beginning. With irony as gentle as a kiss of a mother when she laughs at a child, God called on Job to assume the government of the universe. He told him to take over in the moral realm and try to bring men to the place they ought to be in. He asked him to bring the haughty and the proud low. And He reminded Job that he could not even control some of the animal creation, so his power was limited indeed. The moral problems that had vexed Job were proof to him that he was unable to handle them by himself.

At the end of the first two discourses by the Lord, Job was compelled to face his own incompetence. He could neither control the nonmoral forces nor was he able to control the moral forces, not even those of his own heart.

We are inclined to say that the Lord has been good to us just because we may be prospering financially. But what do we say in the times of adversity? Is the Lord good to us then? In the light of Romans 8:28 no matter what happens we know that all things work together for good to them that love the Lord.

Not so many years ago we had some very severe tests at the Broadcast. They were not only financial, they entered other areas as well. When people met us and asked how God was treating us there was an inner temptation, not necessarily to complain, but to say that things were not going so well. But it was a joy and inspiration based on faith to say, "The Lord is good to us."

I knew that some of these friends thought God must have provided everything that was necessary for us. And for the sake of clarification they would ask me if such were the case. Then I would tell them that was not what I meant. We were passing through many testings and trials but I assured them that I believed God knew what He was doing and that in His own time He would correct these matters for us.

God did not reveal everything about Himself to Job, but He gave him enough information to make faith intelligent despite the persisting dark problems which surrounded him. There is much that we do not know about God. There is much that is unrevealed and kept back from us in order to give faith scope for development. In fact, if we could understand all about God, God would have to be less than we are. However, God is infinitely above us, and as the years come and go He means more to us as we grow in grace and in His knowledge. On the other hand, the more precious He becomes to us personally, the more we realize our incompetence in spiritual things and our inability to grasp the truth concerning God in His fulness.

Job Transformed

The turning point in Job's life was reached when he said, "I know that You can do all things and that no thought or purpose of Yours can be restrained or thwarted. [You said to me] Who is this that darkens and obscures counsel by words without knowledge? Therefore [I now see] I have rashly uttered what I did not understand, things too wonderful for me, which I did not know" (42:2,3).

What a confession this is! What a thorough breakdown! What a profound humbling! Job acknowledged that all his previous statements with regard to God and His ways were words without knowledge. This is a turning point in any man's history when he discovers that he has been all wrong about God and admits it.

There is nothing so hard to confess as our own utter ignorance and fault. When we are under the control of the old nature, this is the last thing we would think of doing. It takes the new nature which each believer receives when he trusts in Christ to enable us to make such confession.

To get right thoughts about God is to begin to get right thoughts about everything. If we are wrong about God we are wrong about ourselves. We will also be wrong about our neighbors and friends. We need to come to the place Job did when he said, "I know thou canst do all things." This was complete surrender and worship. This was the acknowledgment of the absolute sovereign power of Almighty God. With this came renewed faith to give God the right place in Job's own life. He was at the point in his Christian life where Paul later said, "I can do all things through Christ which strengtheneth me."

To acknowledge the absolute sovereignty of God in our lives is to say and mean it that God has the right to do anything He wants to do with us. This is the place we need to come to when passing through trials and sorrows. We do not understand the purpose at the time and the mystery of them may never be revealed this side of glory. We come to the right place in our attitude toward God, however, when we say that He has the right to do anything He wants to do.

Job also acknowledged God's omnipotence. He saw that God had all power and that no purpose of God could be restrained or thwarted. Whatever God wanted to do He had the right to do and no one could stop Him. Here again was a complete surrender, a reversal of all that Job had previously said about God. This was true repentance. No wonder he quoted God and admitted the truth of what God said: "Who is this that darkens and obscures counsel by words without knowledge? Therefore [I now see] I have rashly uttered what I did not understand, things too wonderful for me, which I did not know."

Job had formerly said to Zophar, "I am not inferior to you. What you know, the same things do I know." He was not willing to be thought ignorant by his friends nor was he open to what they might teach him concerning God. They had approached him in the wrong way, treating him as ignorant and presumptuous, calling him a hypocrite and a secret transgressor before God. Nothing will stir up our old nature quicker than for us to be falsely accused. At once there is rebellion, and there is no telling what might happen when the old nature is aroused. (Remember the hippopotamus.) Job would not bow in humility before such men though in his innermost heart he did not want to be a proud man. Still he would not take the humble place before men whose knowledge of God was less than his own. Are we any different?

Brother Ord Morrow who is associate radio minister of the Broadcast used the following illustration when he was pastor of the church where we attended. He told of a young man, a Bible student, who helped him in a certain church during the summer months. When the summer was ended, the young man was about to leave for school again, the two met for prayer.

The student poured out his heart to God saying, "Lord, I am worthless. I am good for nothing. I am so ignorant." And continued on like this for some time.

After they were through praying Mr. Morrow said to him as only he can do it: "Well young man, you worked here for three months and now you are ready to go back to school. No doubt you would like to know what we think of you."

The young man said, "Yes, I would like to know."

So Mr. Morrow went ahead and said, "We think you are good for nothing. We think you are ignorant. . . ." He went on using the same language the young man had used.

The young fellow turned blue, then purple, then white. And finally Mr. Morrow said, "Listen. You know we do not think that about you. You do not even think that of yourself. Then why say to God the things you don't really believe?"

God's Refining of His Saints

There will always be mysteries with regard to the divine counsel of God. Job had at first bowed in humility before God and worshipped even in the face of his greatest losses. But once his friends had come to him with an unjust accusation, he responded by saying things about God that exposed his own ignorance. The Psalmist in contemplating God and His wisdom said, "Such knowledge is too wonderful for me. I cannot comprehend it." This is to be our attitude when we consider God and His ways in our lives. In the refining of gold the heat is kept on the metal until all the dross comes to the top and is cleared away. This was the process God used with Job in a spiritual sense. He allowed the heat of the furnace of affliction to keep on burning until He could see His own image reflected in His servant's heart.

Job had even anticipated this, for during one of the occasions when he was on a high spiritual plane he said, "But he knoweth the way that I take: when he hath tried me, I shall come forth as gold" (23:10, KJV). He was precious in the sight of God even as we are who are His children today. Gold is a perishing element, but the faith of a believer that has been tried by God is far more precious than gold. This is what Peter said in I Peter 1:6,7.

God's chastening of His children is a mark of His love for them. This is what the writer to the Hebrews said: "For whom the Lord loveth he chasteneth" (12:6). God chastens because He loves, not because He hates. He scourges every son whom He receives. None of God's children need expect to avoid the furnace fire of trial, for this is a method

He employs with all members of His family. And we are also told in this same passage in Hebrews that if we endure chastening, God deals with us as sons. The word "sons" in this passage does not only mean that God treats them merely as children, born-again members of His family, but that He treats them as mature, adult sons.

The passage goes on to say that no chastening for the present seems to be joyous but grievous, then it adds this significant phrase: "Nevertheless afterward it yieldeth the peaceable fruit of righteousness unto them which are exercised thereby" (Heb. 12:11).

We see from this that when God permits such things to take place in our lives as He did in Job's life, there is a reason for it. God wants to bring us forth as purified gold.

It is no wonder Job made the acknowledgment he did as this truth began to break upon him. He not only acknowledged that God's purposes could not be thwarted but he said, "I had heard of You only by the hearing of the ear; but now my [spiritual] eye sees You. Therefore I loathe my words and abhor myself, and repent in dust and ashes" (42:5,6). Job had at the beginning only a general knowledge of God. He had been correctly instructed but the knowledge he obtained did not have the personal quality to it that came as a result of the trials through which he passed.

This was true in the case of Jacob. He had a good knowledge of God. He first met Him at Bethel before going on to Haran where he spent 20 years with his uncle. Jacob undoubtedly knew the doctrine of God but one day he met Him in a personal way at Peniel. Through that experience he became more personally acquainted with God and became a much better, yes, a new man as a result of it.

We think of Joshua as a leader of high courage and ability, but at first when the leadership of Israel was given to him he apparently showed signs of fear. God encouraged him and assured him that with God beside him he had nothing to fear. Then one day the Angel of the Lord appeared to him near Jericho and Joshua was never the same man again. He knew God in a much more personal way.

There was a day when God made Himself real to Paul. In his unsaved state, Paul had been a very religious man and very zealous for his religion. In the group he worked with, his zeal for the cause he supported was measured by his persecution of the Christians. He had high moral standards of life so that he could say that he was blameless so far as the outward moral righteousness of the law was concerned, that is as men saw it. But there came a day when all of this was changed. Paul said, "But what things were gain to me, those I counted loss for Christ. Yea doubtless, and I count all things but loss for the excellency of the knowledge of Christ Jesus my Lord: for whom I have suffered the loss of all things, and do count them but dung, that I may win Christ."

Job also had a progressive revelation of God. We have seen evidence of it according to the 40th chapter where Job said he would lay his hand upon his mouth and say nothing more. He saw God in all His holiness and acknowledged His perfect sovereignty. Job admitted that what God did was right.

The patriarch saw himself as incompetent in the moral realm. He was also brought face to face with the fact that he had no control over forces in the nonmoral realm. With the men who had visited him he had more than held his own, but he found that in the presence of God no creature can boast.

Job had a new spiritual comprehension of God which brought a new comprehension of himself. He laid aside self, acknowledging that he was vile. But is this something one must keep on speaking about? Is he to be occupied with his own vileness? We are to make no provision for the flesh the Bible says (Rom. 13:14). Job did not want to do this either, for he said, "I abhor myself." It had taken him a long time to reach this place; but some of us are no quicker than he in getting to this place in our Christian experience, if we ever reach it at all.

Many believers think they have reached the end of themselves when they give mental consent to the doctrine of human depravity and say we are all depraved. But it is one thing to speak of vileness and depravity in general; it is quite another for us to know deep down in our own hearts that we are vile. To say before the Lord, "I am the one," is the place Job came to and the place we need to come to. This is a personal, intimate thing, a private matter between ourselves and God. This is not something that one believer can reveal to another. It comes as the result of the work of the Spirit of God in our hearts.

These two things always go together: "Mine eye seeth thee," and "I abhor myself." To catch a new vision of God and His righteousness is to bring us to the place where we hate what we are in ourselves. When God's light shines into our hearts, we cannot help but abhor ourselves.

Self-abhorrence is seen in a life of self-abnegation. This is expressed by a humble spirit, a lowly mind, a gracious attitude in the midst of the things around us. It is of little use to profess low thoughts of self if we are quick to resent any injury that may be offered us, or to feel insulted when someone has slighted us or discouraged us.

The true secret of a broken and contrite heart is ever to abide in the presence of Almighty God and then to be able to maintain a correct attitude toward those with whom we have to do. This innermost knowledge of God is only given when the soul has been stripped of anything that may dim the vision of God in the heart. There is always the danger of being preoccupied with the blessings of God instead of with God Himself. It is easy to become obsessed with the work of God instead of delighting in the will of God. It is a common fault among us believers to be enamored with the gifts of God such as are outlined in Romans 12 and I Corinthians 12 instead of being occupied with

Christ. We tend to center our attention on the gift instead
of the Giver. It is a common fault among us to be occupied
with the knowledge of God instead of letting that knowledge
carry us forward to knowing God Himself.

Years ago A. B. Simpson wrote of this very weakness
in believers and put it in a form that many of us have sung:

> Once it was the blessing,
>   Now it is the Lord;
> Once it was the feeling,
>   Now it is His Word;
> Once His gift I wanted,
>   Now the Giver own;
> Once I sought for healing,
>   Now Himself alone.
>
> Once it was my working,
>   His it hence shall be;
> Once I tried to use Him,
>   Now He uses me;
> Once the power I wanted,
>   Now the Mighty One;
> Once for self I labored,
>   Now for Him alone.
>
> All in all forever,
>   Jesus will I sing;
> Everything in Jesus,
>   And Jesus everything.

We cannot have the gifts of Christ without having
Him. Yet it is easy to take our eyes off Him and think
only of His gifts.

Job had at last come to know himself and his true
measure. He was satisfied to lie upon his Heavenly Father's
heart and to be content with what He wanted him to be.
At the same time he rejoiced in the gifts and graces that
God gave to others as He saw fit.

It was then that Job said, "I abhor myself." One of

the marginal readings says, "I loathe my words." But the meaning of the Hebrew word is "disappear—I retract, I completely repudiate myself." Previous to this he had said he was vile and of small account. Now he goes much farther. He practically cancels himself out.

He retracted all he had said. He repudiated the position he had taken up. He repented in dust and ashes. The word "repent" here indicates real sorrow. Job said literally, "I cancel myself out. I don't count. I am filled with sorrow."

Job canceled self in the presence of Almighty God. This is exactly what Paul meant when he said, "I am crucified with Christ." This was the negative side that Paul stated and the side that Job had reached. Paul, however, went farther than to say he was canceled out. He added, "Nevertheless, I live; yet not I, but Christ liveth in me." We, including Paul, who live on this side of Calvary, have a blessed privilege not fully enjoyed by those before Calvary. We have the living Christ indwelling us, and this makes possible instant and constant victory. Since Christ is now our life, we by faith may have this victory.

CHAPTER SIXTEEN

JOB VINDICATED BY GOD

Job left the vindication of himself to God. The principle involved here is expressed in Psalm 37:5,6: "Commit thy way unto the Lord; trust also in him; and he shall bring it to pass. And he shall bring forth thy righteousness as the light, and thy judgment as the noonday." We can leave it to God to bring forth our righteous motives and deeds. He will vindicate us if we leave it to Him.

Paul said to the Corinthians when some were criticizing him: "As for me, myself, it is a very little concern to me to be examined by you or any human court; in fact, I do not even examine myself. For although my conscience does not accuse me, yet I am not entirely vindicated by that. It is the Lord Himself who must examine me. So you must stop forming any premature judgments, but wait until the Lord shall come again; for He will bring to light the secrets hidden in the dark and will make known the motives of men's hearts, and the proper praise will be awarded each of us" (I Cor. 4:3-5, Wms.).

This matter of leaving vindication of one's ministry and purpose to the Lord, was one the Lord taught me some years ago. I was often perplexed because not every one wanted to receive the testimony of the Word. There were often letters sent to us that were critical of the ministry. Then the time came when God showed me from Psalm 37 that not only does He lead us and guide us, but that when we follow His directions, He will also vindicate us before others. This is taught in verse 6 which one translation renders: "He will also bring forth as the light thy righteousness, and thy VINDICATION as the noonday."

When any child of God reaches the place Job reached, God lifts him from the dust to a place of fullness of light and glorious experience. God wants us to learn from the difficult circumstances of life that in His wisdom these are for our good and for the furtherance of His work.

Let us now consider in detail how God vindicated Job.

James 5:11 tells us: "Behold, we count them happy which endure. Ye have heard of the patience of Job, and have seen the end of the Lord; that the Lord is very pitiful, and of tender mercy." God does not delight in our being afflicted, yet through these same afflictions His very gracious purposes are realized. This is what James calls "the end of the Lord," and for us as for Job this includes vindication.

The vindication of Job was also a vindication before his friends. God called him "my servant" and had him act in the capacity of a priest for his three friends who had so cruelly slandered him. God's goal in Job's life had been reached, and we have been given this information in order that God might speak to our hearts. The only real purpose of viewing Job at all is to get beyond Job to God. It is not only that we need to see what God was able to do with Job, but we need to see the God of Job for ourselves.

We receive many letters full of distress. Some persons even call me by phone and weep as they describe their situation. They cannot understand all the turmoil and unrest in their lives. They cannot understand why such adverse circumstances surround them. They wonder why God allows it. They and we need to see that God is sovereign throughout His universe. Even Satan cannot thwart the sovereignty of God. God is gracious in His purposes toward us whom He created in His own image. God's gracious purposes toward us persist through all time, even through the most painful trials. These may be mysteries as long as we remain on earth, but we will eventually see their divine purpose.

Always An Afterward

We learn from Job, and this is part of the vindication, that there is always an afterward to the suffering of the godly. There is always a compensation, a reward to come. It may not come in this present life as far as we are concerned. It did in Job's life; but we can be assured that it will eventually come for us. The Bible says so and that settles it. In the case of Job it had to come in his lifetime in order to fill out the object lesson the Lord presented through him. But life for the believer does not end with three-score years and ten if we are spared that long; it continues on into the better land, beyond all earth's sunsets.

For us there is an inheritance reserved in heaven. It is for all who are kept by the power of God.

According to II Timothy 3:12, all who live godly in Christ Jesus will suffer persecution. This does not mean a godly life according to our standards, or a life lived to the best of our ability. The Scriptures are speaking of those of us who have not only accepted Christ by faith but have also appropriated the godly life in Christ Jesus. It is speaking of believers who have allowed Christ to live His life in them. These will suffer persecution for this very reason. It may not always be physical, but the world will persecute the godly in one way or another, for a godly life is a rebuke to the rebellious life. Do we qualify here?

Paul said in II Timothy 2:12, "If we suffer, we shall also reign with him." This is an assurance that though there may be suffering in this life for Christ's sake, in the future we will reign with Him. Look again at I Peter 1:7: "That the trial of your faith, being much more precious than of gold that perisheth, though it be tried with fire, might be found unto praise and honour and glory at the appearing of Jesus Christ." At the Lord's coming, if we have suffered for Him, we will receive praise and honour and glory. Then the passage continues: "Whom having not seen, ye love; in whom, though now ye see him not, yet believing, ye rejoice with joy unspeakable and full of glory: Receiving the end of your faith, even the salvation of your souls" (vv. 8,9). There are three steps in salvation. First of all, there is salvation from the condemnation of sin; then there is salvation from the power or enslavement of sin; and the third step is that which is spoken of in this passage. When we enter His presence at His coming, we will realize the completion of our faith. Then there will be vindication and reward.

In his first letter, Peter wrote a great deal about suffering. He said in 4:12-14: "Beloved, think it not strange concerning the fiery trial which is to try you, as though some strange thing happened unto you: But rejoice, inasmuch as ye are partakers of Christ's sufferings; that, when his glory shall be revealed, ye may be glad also with exceeding joy. If ye be reproached for the name of Christ, happy are ye; for the spirit of glory and of God resteth upon you: on their part he is evil spoken of, but on your part he is glorified." According to this suffering has compensations now, for through it we are made partakers of Christ's sufferings. Then in the future, joy and glory will be added.

James also shed light on the believer's suffering, declaring that they can have present blessing. He wrote: "My brethren, count it all joy when ye fall into divers temptations; Knowing this, that the trying of your faith worketh patience" (James 1:2,3).

We must see, however, that all our rewards are not given in this life. In fact, there may be very few of them in the present life; but we can be sure of them in the future. In the great illustrations of faith given in Hebrews 11 we find that some of the heroes of faith received remarkable rewards in this life. But others again suffered to the death. Here is what the record says: "And others tortured, not accepting deliverance; that they might obtain a better resurrection: And others had trial of cruel mockings and scourgings, yea, moreover of bonds and imprisonment: They were stoned, they were sawn asunder, were tempted, were slain with the sword: they wandered about in sheepskins and goatskins; being destitute, afflicted, tormented" (vv. 35-37).

These were heroes of faith as were those mentioned before them. God was making gold out of them. The fiery trials made it possible for Him to see His image in them. But there was something more in connection with them. The last two verses of Hebrews 11 tell us: "And these all, having obtained a good report through faith, received not the promise: God having provided some better thing for us, that they without us should not be made perfect" (vv. 39,40). The day is coming when God will reward these who have waited so long for it. They have not yet received it, because He wants to include us with them in that reward giving.

"The End of the Lord"

People often ask if it pays to be a Christian. They even wonder if it pays to believe in God when they see some families or individuals passing through deep trials, perhaps involving very tragic deaths. God's word has the answer: "Behold, we count them happy which endure. Ye have heard of the patience [endurance] of Job, and have seen the end of the Lord; that the Lord is very pitiful, and of tender mercy" (James 5:11). The expression "the end of the Lord" is used in connection with Job and this is what we see in the portion of the Book we are now in. The end of the Lord is something to wonder at and to rejoice in. It was the end of the Lord that brought about Job's complete transformation, his vindication, and finally

his restoration. Paradise lost became Paradise regained for
the godly sufferer.

The point we have reached in our studies shows Job
to be a sick man and still sitting on an ash heap. His body
is full of sores and undoubtedly the leprosy or whatever
disease it was had changed his appearance until he looked
repulsive. When he spoke of repenting in dust and ashes,
he was literally sitting on dust and ashes.

Though God had undertaken Job's vindication, He gave
His servant no promise that a change in his physical condition or economic condition would result from his changed
attitude. So, Job still had some tests ahead.

Wrong Attitudes of the Friends

The Lord made Job's three friends come to him in order
to make themselves right with God and with Job. It was
not only that they needed to change their attitude toward
God. They needed to make things right with this man whom
they had so unjustly suspected and grievously maligned.
This is what the Lord said to them: "And it was so, that
after the Lord had spoken these words unto Job, the Lord
said to Eliphaz the Temanite, My wrath is kindled against
thee, and against thy two friends: for ye have not spoken
of me the thing that is right, as my servant Job hath"
(42:7, KJV). It may surprise some that the Lord's wrath
was kindled against these men. There is no reason for such
surprise, however, when we remember that they more
nearly wrecked Job's soul than the Devil himself had been
able to do. When Satan had done his very worst, Job's
response was such that he "sinned not, nor charged God
foolishly" (1:22, KJV). Even after the second test when
Job's body had been greatly afflicted, the record is: "In
all this did not Job sin with his lips" (2:10, KJV).

It was because of these so-called friends who had
piously misrepresented both God and Job that the poor
sufferer allowed himself to be driven into sinning with

his lips. Their lack of love did him more harm in some respects than the other things he had endured. What they may have considered to be honest admonition delivered in a zeal for truth was actually unkind and untruthful and entirely void of love.

We know from I Corinthians 13 that eloquence without love is useless. All three so-called friends were eloquent but were harmful rather than useful. Love is kind, but they were not kind. Love is not boastful or vainglorious. The friends of Job showed no hesitancy in telling what they knew or thought they knew.

Love thinks no evil, yet these men thought evil of Job. They left no room in their thinking for any other possible interpretation than the one they made that Job was receiving his just deserts. Love is not conceited about its own goodness but is ever ready to believe the best concerning others.

We must remember that God did not write this Book of Job for history's sake but for our sakes. If we do not learn from it, we will eventually find that we have turned our back on truth God has intended for us to live by.

Satan had no more dangerous tool than these so-called friends of Job. Under the guise of piety and in the name of religious orthodoxy they offered false comfort and gave untrue impressions of God. It would have been far better for them to have been silent in the presence of suffering than to have said the wrong things they did.

Wrong Views of the Friends

God addressed Himself to Eliphaz who apparently was the spokesman for the group and possibly their accepted leader. God said Eliphaz and his friends had not spoken the thing that was right. They had asserted that God's wrath was against Job and that God was punishing Job for his sins. In reality it was as a refiner of gold that God dealt with Job, applying the fire until the spiritual dross was removed. This was God's purpose in Job's suffering. The friends' conclusions were altogether wrong. They even tried to use Job's suffering as a proof that God was against him.

They also tried to make it appear that they were contending for God's righteousness and were zealous for His honor. They saw, however, when God's wrath was kindled against them, that He will not accept honor at the expense of truth. Men often do; and the old nature within us will encourage us to do so also, but God is against it. With God honor and truth must blend into one harmonious light. God is light. This speaks of absolute righteousness; thus it would be impossible for Him to accept honor at the expense of truth.

This is a danger that is as real now as it was then. It is possible for people who love the Lord to be zealous of His honor and yet distort truth by presenting half-truths, thereby tearing down the character of others who also may love the Lord. Half-truths do not come from God. He is not back of this kind of thing any more than He would accept honor at the expense of truth from these friends of Job. Would we expect God to accept a vindication of His character and ways based upon a false charge? Never! This would be to put the stigma of wickedness and hypocrisy upon a man of whom the Lord Himself declared that there was none like him in all the earth, a perfect and an upright man, one who feared God and hated evil. Neither could God endorse such false assumptions as suffering is always for wickedness, and suffering is always an evidence of God's wrath against the sufferer.

If such were the case, then what becomes of God's testing of His own children? Where would we have the right to speak of the sanctifying effect of the chastenings of God? Thus we see that these men were actually defaming the character of God Himself. He could not accept this nor could He allow these men to go unrebuked. He would have nothing to do with them until they made this matter right by confession and sacrifice. Sacrifice and confession involved not only God but Job also, since they had wronged him so greatly.

This then, was part of God's way of vindicating Job. It was also God's way of bringing these men back into proper relationship with Himself. They had to accept Job as a priest on their behalf before God. This is the end of the Lord. This is the way God treats us when we recognize Him as Job did, and are tried as gold purified through fire as Job was. When a man's ways please the Lord, even his enemies are made to be at peace with him. God has promised to vindicate us who are His children when we walk in His paths.

Eliphaz had been guilty of asserting that his knowledge had been obtained through a direct revelation from God. The Lord, however, repudiated the whole teaching of Eliphaz. The Lord refused to be identified with the spirit and the spirit voice and what the spirit taught. God said in effect that what the spirit said did not come from Him. Satan had come as an angel of light to Eliphaz and through him was hoping to cause Job to renounce his faith.

In these last days we must be alert to the danger of strange spirits and revelations. It is not uncommon for some who claim to know the Lord to say they have a revelation from Him, that God spoke to them and told them so and so. But is this in harmony with God's Word? If what they say is true to the Bible then we can accept it— not because they say it but because the Bible teaches it. If it is not according to the Scriptures, it is not the Holy Spirit speaking. We are told to "prove the spirits whether they be of God." We have the complete Word of God and do not need any new revelation.

So these men were sent to Job and instructed as to the kind of sacrifice they were to make. God was not ashamed to be called Job's God and spoke of Job as His servant. Thus God vindicated the man who abhorred himself, who was considered an outcast by his friends and was the song of the drunkards. God spoke of him possessively as "my servant Job." Does it pay us to follow the Lord? Of course it does! This is the end of the Lord who is full of mercy.

What do you think will be Christ's acknowledgment of us in that day when we stand before Him at His appearing? What will be the "end of the Lord" in our case? Will it be, "Well done, thou good and faithful servant: thou hast been faithful over a few things, I will make thee ruler over many things: enter thou into the joy of thy Lord"? (Matt. 25:21). Or will it be as the Lord said to another: "Thou wicked and slothful servant, thou knewest that I reap where I sowed not, and gather where I have not strawed: Thou oughtest therefore to have put my money to the exchangers . . . . Take therefore the talent from him, and give it unto him which hath . . . . And cast ye the unprofitable servant into outer darkness: there shall be weeping and gnashing of teeth"? (Matt. 25:26-30).

The Lord is coming again and that coming could be soon. We are to watch, for we do not know what hour our Lord may come. Therefore it is necessary that we always be ready (Matt. 24:42,44).

According to Matthew 16:27 the Son of Man is going to come in the glory of His Father with His angels and He will reward every man according to his works. One of the last promises in the last chapter of the Bible is concerned with this same truth: "And, behold, I come quickly; and my reward is with me, to give every man according as his work shall be" (Rev. 22:12). No wonder when Peter considered the end times he said, "What manner of persons ought ye to be in all holy conversation and godliness."

Job Spoke What Was Right

These studies in Job are more than a mere character study of a man. God had them written for our admonition. He did not portray the whole life of Job, only a brief but very significant part of it. We know little about Job's early life. He is introduced as a rich and prosperous man, and a man blessed with ten children. He had everything this world could offer, and was regarded as the greatest man of the East.

The main part of the Book covers but a few months at the most of Job's life. They were months of intense suffering which were followed by spiritual results that can be summed up as we have already seen: transformation, vindication and restoration. Then a very brief statement at the end of the book covers the rest of Job's life, a period of 140 years.

In the vindication of His servant God said that Job had spoken what was right. Our first reaction might be to wonder if we read the words correctly, for Job said some things he very much regretted. The problem is really no problem, because God did not refer to the bitter charges Job made against Him. Job had been restored to communion with God. His foolish words were all under the blood, as we say. They were forgiven. When God forgives something He forgets it. Thus God was not referring to Job's rash statements.

God did not even include the wonderful statements Job made in the intervals of deep faith which punctuated his time of trial. Among other things he said, "Though he slay me, yet will I trust in him," and "I know that my redeemer liveth." These are remarkable statements of faith but God did not refer to them. What He had in mind was what Job said in answer to His dealings with him: "I know thou canst do everything and that no thought can be withholden from thee. I have heard of thee with the hearing of the ear: but now mine eye seeth thee. Wherefore I abhor myself, and repent in dust and ashes." In this he had let God be God. He had testified that God is the Self-Existent One, the Perfect One, the All-Wise, the Just, the Righteous One as well as the All-Powerful One. Job acknowledged that God is righteous, and is holy in all His ways. Whether

He sends clouds or sunshine, His name is blessed! This is the conclusion Job reached, and this is what the Lord had reference to.

The Psalmist said, "Wait on the Lord, and keep his way, and he shall exalt thee to inherit the land: when the wicked are cut off, thou shalt see it. I have seen the wicked in great power, and spreading himself like a green bay tree. Yet he passed away, and, lo, he was not: yea, I sought him, but he could not be found. Mark the perfect man [the man whose heart is set on God with singleness of eye, that is singleness of purpose], and behold the upright: for the end of that man is peace" (Ps. 37:34-37).

In another place David declared: "Bless the Lord, O my soul: and all that is within me, bless his holy name. Bless the Lord, O my soul, and forget not all his benefits: Who forgiveth all thine iniquities; who healeth all thy diseases; Who redeemeth thy life from destruction; who crowneth thee with loving kindness and tender mercies; Who satisfieth thy mouth with good things; so that thy youth is renewed like the eagle's. The Lord executeth righteousness and judgment for all that are oppressed" (Ps. 103:1-6). This is in essence what Job had said.

It is no wonder, then, that God commanded Job's friends to take seven bullocks and seven rams and offer up a burnt offering and Job would pray for them. God said He would accept Job's prayer but not theirs, for they had not spoken of God the thing that was right as had Job. Seven is the number of perfection, so this sacrifice indicated the need of a full and complete sacrifice for the evil these men had done. Moreover, they had to humble themselves by going to Job in order that he might pray for them. God did not say that He would not accept the prayers of these friends afterwards, but at that time He would not hear them apart from Job's intercession. By obeying God in this, they admitted they had wronged Job. This was God's way of vindicating His servant before his friends. At the same time this brought them to lowliness and humility. Poor, misunderstood Job was not lost sight of.

How complete had been the rebuke and how gracious the restoration! God was tender in dealing with Job in it all. How often has this kind of thing been repeated in the history of the children of God. Joseph, for example, was ill-treated by his brethren, sold into slavery, then exalted in Egypt. Years later God brought Joseph's brethren to Egypt, and they bowed in submission to the brother they had sought to harm. He in graciousness forgave them and tenderly cared for them.

I recall an incident that is very close to my heart. Years ago when I was a young pastor, a man in the congregation for some reason became my bitter enemy. He went out of his way to rebuke me and said things about me that were untrue. His dislike increased to where he finally said I was not ever to visit him again. This was no ordinary animosity. I could do nothing with this situation except commit it to the Lord's care.

Eventually we moved from the community and did not return for a visit until several years had elapsed. In the course of my visit I was told that this man had just been brought home from the hospital and was not expected to live. I knew I must once again go to see him and attempt to reestablish fellowship with him. I went to his bedside wondering if his attitude had changed any in the meantime. My first words to him were, "My, what a place to find you."

He stretched out his hand to me and answered: "This is where God has put me to meet you." He took hold of my hand and held it for some 30 minutes. He asked me to pray for him as he poured out his heart in contrition. What a sacred moment in my own life—we were reconciled before our next meeting in glory.

This is a valuable lesson for us as believers. The Lord tells us through James that if we humble ourselves before

Him, He will give us the needed grace for whatever situation we find ourselves in (James 4:6). In Matthew 23:12 there is both a warning and a blessing given by the Saviour Himself: "Whosoever shall exalt himself shall be abased; and he that shall humble himself shall be exalted."

A Three-Fold Lesson

There is a remarkable three-fold lesson in this incident in Job 42 with reference to prayer. This does not belong exclusively to Job's experience, for the principles found here are basic to all true prayer.

First of all, God said to the three friends that Job would pray for them. How did God know this? The reason is that true prayer begins with God. The impression must come from Him. The desire and the longing have to find their source in Him. Job was now in such complete submission to God and so completely at His disposal that God was able to put it into his heart to pray for his friends. Job was so completely under God's control that anything He wanted him to do he would do without hesitation. True prayer begins with God and is expressed through a heart obedient to God.

The second principle is seen in God's promise to accept Job's prayer on behalf of the friends. This is the wonderful truth that a God-inspired prayer will always be accepted by Him. We learn from Romans 8:26,27: "Likewise the Spirit also helpeth our infirmities: for we know not what we should pray for as we ought: but the Spirit [Himself] maketh intercession for us with groanings which cannot be uttered. And he that searcheth the hearts [this is the Almighty God, I believe] knoweth what is the mind of the Spirit, because he maketh intercession for the saints according to the will of God."

The third principle is seen where God turned the captivity of Job when he prayed for his friends. When our sole purpose is God's glory, then God will prosper us in one way or another. In II Chronicles 16:9 we read: "For the eyes of the Lord run to and fro throughout the whole earth, to show himself strong in behalf of them whose heart is perfect toward him."

So it was, then, that the Lord turned the captivity of Job, when he prayed for his friends. This to me is one of the most wonderful things I have read in the whole Book of Job. It is a rare and exquisite fruit of divine workmanship. Nothing can be more touching than to see Job's three friends exchanging their former experiences, their traditions and their legality for the grace which came from offering the burnt offerings. Then we see Job exchanging his bitter denunciations for the sweet prayer of love. In short, this is the most soul-subduing scene that one could witness. These men are in the dust before God and at the same time are in each others arms. The strife is over. The war of words is ended. Instead, we have tears of repentance, the sweet odor of burnt offering and the embrace of love. What a happy scene! Precious fruits of the divine ministry!

CHAPTER SEVENTEEN

JOB RESTORED

What more is needed? What but that the Lord Himself should lay the capstone on a beautiful structure like this. And this is exactly what the Lord did. We read that He "gave Job twice as much as he had before." (42:10). But how was this done? What agency did God use? Or did Job do it by his own independent industry and clever management, matters he had spoken of previously. No. All was changed. Job had a new heart attitude. He had new thoughts about God, about himself, about his friends, and about his circumstances. All things had become new as we read in II Corinthians 5:17: "If any man be in Christ . . . old things are passed away; behold, all things are become new." Job, of course, had been saved for a long time; he was now developing more spiritually.

Job received God's promise of having his goods restored, but the method of how this was to be done he left to the Lord. Here is how that work began: "Then came there unto him all his brethren, and all his sisters, and all they that had been of his acquaintance before, and did eat bread with him in his house: and they bemoaned him, and comforted him over all the evil [afflictions] that the Lord had brought upon him: every man also gave him a piece of money, and every one an earring of gold" (42:11, KJV).

God had His own way of doing things for Job. Why not let God be God in our lives also? Let Him do as He wills, and let Him do it in His own way. Perhaps someone who is suffering says, "I wish it were that way with me. If I could see good health, and have prosperity, and have dear ones restored to me here and now, I would be satisfied."

If this is our attitude, consider these facts. Do we realize that we as believers have blessings Job did not have? We have greater spiritual riches than he ever anticipated. Paul wrote in Ephesians 1:3: "Blessed be the God and Father of our Lord Jesus Christ, who hath blessed us with all spiritual blessings in heavenly places in Christ." Later on in the same chapter he wrote that we have been sealed by the Holy Spirit who is the earnest of our inheritance until the redemption of the purchased possession (vv. 13,14). Being sealed by the Spirit of God is something Job did not have. Consider also the truth given in Hebrews 10: 36,37: "For ye have need of patience, that, after ye have done the will of God, ye might receive the promise. For yet a little while, and he that shall come will come, and will not tarry."

Another part of our riches is made known in II Corinthians 4:16-18: "For which cause we faint not; but though our outward man perish, yet the inward man is renewed day by day. For our light affliction, which is but for a moment, worketh for us a far more exceeding and eternal weight of glory; While we look not at the things which are seen, but at the things which are not seen: for the things which are seen are temporal; but the things which are not seen are eternal."

Then Paul tells us in Romans 8:17,18 that we are joint-heirs with Christ. Because we are joint-heirs with Christ we shall be glorified together with Him. Then the apostle adds: "For I reckon that the sufferings of this present time are not worthy to be compared with the glory which shall be revealed in us."

Job's Tests Not Over

Let us now look at some of the lessons to be learned from Job's restoration. First of all, the Bible does not say that the Lord restored all Job's possessions and then Job prayed for his friends. It says when Job had prayed for his friends, the Lord restored him to and beyond his former prosperity. The Lord revealed Himself to His servant, rebuked the so-called friends, and acknowledged Job as belonging to Him. But Job was still an afflicted man, destitute of all that he once possessed. He was homeless, seemingly friendless, a mere beggar upon an ash heap.

Surely we would think Job needed prayer for himself before he would pray for his accusers. That, at least, is the way the natural man or the carnal Christian would think, for the man controlled by the Adamic nature thinks of self only. Job had undergone a remarkable transformation. Self had been recognized as crucified and was therefore canceled out. When Paul stated: "I am crucified with Christ" he used the tense that meant this act took place when Jesus was crucified. So far as the results in our lives are concerned, however, this means that we are now crucified with Christ.

Job's tests were not all ended. At least two more are indicated in this last chapter in the Book of Job. God said Job would pray for his friends and God would accept his prayer. Yet these very things could have given the self-life in Job a new opportunity for expression. The Lord permitted this as a test to show that Job was living as one dead to sin and self but alive to God. This meant Job saw that his relationship to God was first, then to others, and to himself last.

How much more should this be true in us when we reckon on the fact that our position in Christ is one of perfection. In our time, which is after the resurrection of Christ, we have Him in us, living out His life through us. This is what Paul meant when he said, "I am crucified with Christ: nevertheless I live; yet not I, but Christ liveth in me." Job had ceased putting his affairs first and attended to the needs of others ahead of his own.

What in Job's day was the correct attitude to follow after, is now much more complete, for now we are complete in Christ. That is, Christ is our all in all. Certainly, we have no excuse for failure because we read in Colossians 2:9,10: "For in him [Christ] dwelleth all the fullness of the Godhead bodily. And ye are complete in him."

Think also of Ephesians 2:4-6: "But God . . . even when we were dead in sins, hath quickened us together with Christ, (by grace ye are saved;) And hath raised us up together, and made us sit together in heavenly places in Christ Jesus."

Since we are in Christ Jesus, we are in the position of absolute victory. It is from this position of victory that we go forward. Job was working toward this position of victory looking forward by faith to Christ's death. God in His mercy gave His servant grace to see that the old self was as good as crucified although Jesus had not yet been crucified. God released Job from the domination of his Adamic nature when His servant allowed Him to do so. The new life in Job was due to the Holy Spirit living out that life in him.

Some may ask, "Are these would-be comforters who dealt so harshly with Job to be thought of first? Is this the way God wanted it?" Or Job may have asked: "Are they to be pardoned and blessed before I am, whom God has acknowledged as His servant? Is there to be no deliverance for me?"

Some might say that he had a right to think in this fashion. But so far as we know he did not. At least there is no record of it. Instead, when these persons came to Job, though he was outwardly still a beggar, he acted like a prince having power with God. This reminds us of Jacob's experience at Peniel when he met God and the Lord blessed him, changing his name from a schemer who put self interests first, to Israel, a prince with God.

There was another test. Not only did Job pray for his friends, but if his prayer was to be answered and accepted of God, it had to be a prayer with earnest, honest desire. It was not to be a matter of mere words. He might have come as children do quite often and submit because they feel they have no other recourse. But this prayer had to be something from the heart, something that Job really wanted. Was it his all-consuming desire to see these men forgiven and blessed, these who had misjudged him so cruelly and dealt with him so harshly? Were they to be forgiven while he was left upon an ash heap outside the village? Could he really pray for such a blessing to come to them under these circumstances?

Job prayed so that his prayer prevailed before God. In Mark 11:24 our Lord said, "Therefore I say unto you, What things soever ye desire, when ye pray, believe that ye receive them, and ye shall have them."

Here was a man who prayed as Jesus prayed when evil men nailed Him to a cross: "Father, forgive them; for they know not what they do." Our Lord thought of others in His hour of agony.

When men stoned Stephen he prayed for them: "Lord, lay not this sin to their charge." The same Jesus who accomplished this through Stephen is able to do the same through us if we will allow Him. We must believe that we have been crucified with Christ and that Christ now is living in us.

When was victory completely won in Job's life? I am sure it was completed when he said, "I abhor myself, and repent in dust and ashes." But it was not until God put this new life to the test and Job prayed for his friends that the Lord restored him.

So it will be with us in the experiences of life. When we leave self in the hands of God and let Christ's mind control us, the Lord will bring us into the place of blessing.

The Double Portion

With regard to Job's blessings following his time of great trial we learn "the Lord gave Job twice as much as he had before" (42:10, KJV). This was a double portion of blessing. We can see this very clearly when we compare the numbers of animals Job had before his trials set in with the numbers after his trials were over. But a problem arises with regard to his children. The record is, "He had also seven sons and three daughters" (v. 13, KJV). This is the exact number he had before. His economic benefits were doubled, but if the statement in verse 10 included his children, the only explanation I can offer is that he had not lost his first seven sons and three daughters; they had just gone on to glory before him. Then, God gave him seven more sons and three more daughters, making 20 in all.

The double portion God gave Job is rich in spiritual content. It can be illustrated from II Kings 2 in an incident involving Elijah and Elisha. Elijah was to be taken to heaven, and after he and Elisha crossed the Jordan River, Elijah said: "Ask what I shall do for thee, before I be taken away from thee."

Elisha's answer was, "I pray thee, let a double portion of thy spirit be upon me." Elisha had passed the test which proved him worthy of receiving a so-called double portion. This does not mean that he would have twice as much of the Holy Spirit as Elijah had. The Spirit of God is a person so this is not what is meant. The reference is to a custom in Israel where the first-born received as his birthright a double portion of the inheritance. This, of course, had to do with a family estate, but Elisha used the expression with a spiritual meaning.

Elijah said to him, "Thou hast asked a hard thing: nevertheless, if thou see me when I am taken from thee, it shall be so unto thee; but if not, it shall not be so" (II

Kings 2:10). Then we are told, Elijah went up by a whirl-wind into heaven and Elisha saw it.

In what respect was this a hard thing that Elisha had asked? It was hard because suffering was involved. How-ever, so far as Elisha was concerned, it was apparent he had already passed the test.

Job too had passed the test. He had found victory over self so that he had the right of a firstborn to the birthright.

The birthright of the believer is in Christ, but it is something we enjoy only as self is put in its proper place. The doctrinal aspect of this is in Romans 6 as we have pointed out previously in these studies. We are to take our place as those who are crucified with Christ and, there-fore, dead unto sin but alive unto God through Jesus Christ our Lord.

This does not mean that the old nature is removed. It is still there but is conquered through Christ in us. This is possible only through faith. According to the 7th chapter of Romans, Paul apparently tried to find victory in himself but met defeat until he found deliverance was in Christ. The 8th chapter of Romans is the chapter of victory.

Christ is the "Firstborn" of God. The birthright is His. But since we are children, we are also "heirs of God, and joint-heirs with Christ; if so be that we suffer with him" (Rom. 8:17). In what way are we to suffer? This does not necessarily mean physical suffering though it could be. It means to suffer the loss of all things as Paul did so as to be brought to the end of the self-life. (See Phil. 3:7-9.)

We learn from Ephesians 2:6 that we have been raised up together and made to sit together in heavenly places in Christ Jesus. Our Lord has already received His position because of His birthright, and we are potentially seated with Him in the heavenlies. We enjoy the blessing of it when we, like Paul, count all things but loss for the ex-cellency of the knowledge of Christ Jesus our Lord (Phil. 3:8).

While Job had known the power of the Holy Spirit in his life and work previous to his great trial, through the trial he had been led from faith to faith. God wanted to make of him a fit vessel and to provide him with a double portion, which he eventually enjoyed. It was through suffering that Job came to this place; and it is through suffering of one type or another that we are brought to the same place. So one of the blessings of suffering to us is that we might receive the benefits of the double portion.

It is a common experience among human beings for those who are in trouble to find themselves without friends, and those who are being prospered to have many "friends." While Job was in the midst of his suffering, he had no comfort from the people he had known and from his relatives who should have offered him sympathy. Then after he was restored, they came around and provided him with gifts.

This was another test for Job. He had been a successful business man who was not inclined to take gifts from others. This is the attitude some persons have toward salvation. If it costs them nothing, if it is free, as the Scripture says, they do not want it. Anything they get they want to pay for. But Job's self-pride was broken so that he could without hesitation receive things from others. Since this was God's method of helping him, then it was good.

A great tragedy with many persons is that they will not accept the truth of their complete depravity. This is the reason they will not, on the other hand, accept a free salvation. This is why the majority of so-called Christians are hard at work today trying to save themselves.

But what about those of us who have been gloriously saved? We have accepted our position as being totally depraved in sin and know Christ is our only Saviour. Are we now guilty of trying to work out our own salvation in a sense that God did not tell us to? In other words, have

we trusted Christ for salvation's beginning but work as
though the continuation of our salvation depended upon
our efforts? The salvation we are to work out is the salvation God has already wrought in us.

We must come to the place with regard to our Christian
walk where we acknowledge that we cannot cope with
the self nature nor improve it in any way, shape or form.
We must come to the place where we realize we have no
power in ourselves to do the work and will of God. Until
we reach that place we will never qualify for the birthright God has for us. We are instructed in Colossians 2:6:
"As ye have therefore received Christ Jesus the Lord, so
walk ye in him." We received Him by faith and we are
to continue the Christian walk through faith. This is the
same truth taught in Romans 1:17 where we are instructed
to go from faith to faith. Peter adds to this when he tells
us in his Second Letter that God has given us all things
essential for our salvation and for our daily Christian
walk. All that is needed is Christ in us the hope of glory
(II Peter 1:3,4; Col. 1:27).

More on the End of the Lord

"The end of the Lord" is a phrase we have already
investigated at some length, but so far as Job is concerned
there is more about it that we should see. We read in the
last two verses of this great Book: "After this lived Job
an hundred and forty years, and saw his sons, and his
sons' sons, even four generations. So Job died, being old
and full of days" (42:16,17, KJV). A period of 140 years
is a long time in itself, but Job lived this following the
time of his great trial. No doubt he had more trials and
testings which would only be normal, but he also went
on to live to a ripe old age.

During the time of his sorrows he might have thought
his life was full of nights. But now because of the "end
of the Lord" Job's years were "full of days." It was always

days—days of sunshine even though there were times of darkness along the way, but the dark times would be brief. Undoubtedly Job had learned what the Psalmist described when he said, "If I say, Surely the darkness shall cover me; even the night shall be light about me. Yea, the darkness hideth not from thee; but the night shineth as the day: the darkness and light are both alike to thee. For thou hast possessed my reins: thou hast covered me in my mother's womb" (Ps. 139:11-13).

We could not do better in closing this portion of our study than to repeat the prayer of the Psalmist: "Search me, O God, and know my heart: try me, and know my thoughts: And see if there be any wicked way in me, and lead me in the way everlasting" (Ps. 139:23,24).

POSTSCRIPT ON SUFFERING

The Book of Job has approached suffering mainly from this one angle: "Why do the righteous suffer?" But there is suffering in this world that stems from many causes and has many purposes. God permitted Job to suffer in order to bring him to a high degree of spiritual refinement. His suffering was not punishment but disciplinary. It was not judgment but educative, designed to produce spiritual development.

The Bible reveals many other causes for suffering. It is not uncommon for example, that a Christian suffers by reason of his own sins. This, of course, was not the case with Job; but it is something to be expected since a man, no matter who he is, reaps what he sows. The slothful servant suffered the loss of all he had. He did not qualify for rewards. His pound was taken from him and given to him who had ten pounds. The principle the Lord laid down was, "Unto everyone that hath shall be given; and from him that hath not, even that which he hath shall be taken away." This is God's order in things. So we must be careful not to misinterpret the reason for our suffering when we pass through such periods.

In his First Letter Peter took up the subject of suffering in some detail. He wrote: "Beloved, think it not strange concerning the fiery trial which is to try you, as though some strange thing happened unto you: But rejoice, inasmuch as ye are partakers of Christ's sufferings; that, when his glory shall be revealed, ye shall be glad also with exceeding joy" (4:12,13). This was the kind of suffering Job endured.

"If ye be reproached for the name of Christ, happy are ye; for the spirit of glory and of God resteth upon you: on their part he is evil spoken of, but on your part he is glorified" (v. 14). Such is the result in the life of every believer who has had to pass through persecution for his or her faith in Christ.

"But let none of you suffer as a murderer, or as a thief, or as an evildoer, or as a busybody in other men's matters" (v. 15). It is a good thing to suffer for Christ's sake, but it is an evil thing when we suffer because of wrongdoing on our part. The apostle begins this list of evildoers with a murderer and ends up with a gossiper. If we do any of the things mentioned here we need not think we are suffering for the cause of Christ. We deserve the judgment that falls on us in such a case.

In verse 16 Peter says, "Yet if any man suffer as a Christian, let him not be ashamed; but let him glorify God on this behalf." Job was like this. He was mature and God's glory was clearly brought out at the end. The Lord speaks of Job as being blameless—not sinless. So if any of us are going to benefit from suffering as Job did, there will have to be a certain degree of maturity evident in our lives.

We learn from I Corinthians 10:13 that no temptation or testing has taken us but such as is common to man. "But God is faithful who will not suffer you to be tempted above that ye are able; but will with the temptation also make a way of escape, that ye may be able to bear it." These testings are designed to produce maturity and growth. Then, as we endure more of this type of suffering, there will be a greater reward following. We can also rest assured that in the midst of the testing there is a way of escape. It may not necessarily be the removal of the test. But if God does not remove it, He will give grace for it.

Just as there are degrees of suffering there are also degrees of reward. Some of us suffer in only one or two ways that Job suffered. These are permitted according to our need and maturity. Some of us lose earthly possessions but nothing else. Others of us may lose loved ones. Others among us may lose health. Some are bedridden and cannot do the service of the Lord they once were able to perform.

God knows what we are and what we can endure; He will not allow us to be tested beyond our ability. He knows our temperaments and dispositions. He knows our various characteristics, our strong points and weak points; therefore He knows what to allow in our lives.

I have often heard people try to explain some of their lapses and actions by saying that their problem is their nature. The trouble is that they are talking about their old fallen nature and there is no good thing in it. But why cater to that nature? Why excuse ourselves on that basis? This is often the reason why God allows suffering in our lives —He wants to show us the way of victory, the way of conquering our old nature.

It may be that we will be facing certain dangers in life, so God allows certain trials to come to us beforehand to prepare us for these dangers. If our suffering is for wrongs done by us, then let us confess them to the Lord and ask God to clean house for us.

On the other hand, when it is suffering due to false accusations made against us, or suffering unjustly in some way or another, let us praise God. Through it He is preparing us for something greater in the future.

I recall a time during my student days in seminary that I could not find a job. Others landed jobs but I did not. At the time I did not know what God was teaching me; but now I know He taught me in those days how to pray and trust Him for funds. He was preparing me ahead of time for the work He has me in now.

There are some people who are always on the go. Sometimes the Lord has to shut such persons up for awhile before He can get any chance to reach their hearts. I think there was something of this in Elijah. One of the hardest things I believe he had to do was wait day in and day out by a brook and later on spend months in the home of a poor widow. He could not get out into active work. This was God's way of teaching him to be completely committed to Him alone. In my estimation this was a period of suffering in some ways for Elijah.

Some do not like to wait on God's time. They run ahead of Him. Moses, though a godly man, showed a tendency in this way in the first part of his adult life. He wanted to do the Lord's will. He knew that Israel was to be emancipated during his lifetime, and he apparently realized that God had trained him for this work. But he ran ahead of God. The Lord had to take him to the desert for a period of 40 years in order to prepare him for his future responsibilities.

God Is in Control

We must always remember that God is in complete control in our suffering. The Devil can only go so far. We cannot be stripped of salvation even during an hour of deep testing. We may wonder at times how we can stand up under some trials, but God has promised He will never let us out of His hands. Our Saviour said in John 10:27,28: "My sheep hear my voice, and I know them, and they follow me: And I give unto them eternal life; and they shall never perish." This is a wonderful promise. In it God guarantees to keep our salvation. This is His responsibility, not ours. But not only that, the Lord went on to say, "and no man shall pluck them out of my hand." Not even the Devil can pluck us out of the hand of Almighty God. In this our Lord was no doubt referring to times of deep trials.

Peter emphasizes this in his First Letter where he says We "are kept by the power of God through faith" (1:5). This means that we cannot take ourselves out of God's hand. God is faithful, He will not deny Himself. We can trust Him to take care of us.

Suffering has benefits in the future. According to II Timothy 2:12: "If we suffer, we shall also reign with him: if we deny him, he also will deny us." That is, God will deny us the reward because we refuse to suffer with Christ. Yet the same passage goes on to assure us that "if we believe not [if our faith should fail], yet he abideth faithful: he cannot deny himself" (v. 13).

God Is Always on Time

God is never too late in coming to our aid but is always on time. In our impatience we may think there has been a delay, but in reality God always acts at the right moment. In Hebrews 4:16 we read: "Let us therefore come boldly unto the throne of grace, that we may obtain mercy, and find grace to help in the time of need." G. Campbell Morgan pointed that the expression "in time of need" is an idiom which could be translated "in the nick of time." God does not necessarily act when we think he should, but He always does it at the right time. If there are seeming delays, it is in order that glory will be brought to Him.

A good illustration of this principle is found in Mark 6. After the Lord had fed the 5000 we are told that He "constrained his disciples to get into the ship, and to go to the other side before unto Bethsaida, while he sent away the people. And when he had sent them away, he departed into a mountain to pray" (vv. 45,46).

When evening came the ship was in the middle of the sea and the Saviour was on the land. This was the time when the Enemy had a chance at them. But "he [Christ] saw them toiling in rowing; for the wind was contrary unto them: and about the fourth watch of the night he cometh unto them, walking upon the sea, and would have passed by them. But when they saw him walking upon the sea, they supposed it had been a spirit, and cried out: For they all saw him, and were troubled. And immediately he talked with them and saith unto them, Be of good cheer: it is I; be not afraid. And he went unto them into the ship; and the wind ceased: and they were sore amazed in themselves beyond measure, and wondered" (vv. 48-51).

According to this record our Saviour saw the disciples in distress but He delayed in going to their aid. It was not until three o'clock in the morning that He went to their rescue. Why did He allow them to battle the waves all that time? He was teaching them a lesson, though we are not told what that particular lesson was. He did not arrive too late to help them, however. He arrived in the nick of time. Whatever else was involved in this, the disciples learned to know Him a little better, finding out that in the seeming delays there is a divine purpose.

We like them need to learn to trust Him; and as Paul said, we also need to learn to know Him. "Cast not away therefore your confidence, which hath great recompence of reward. For ye have need of patience, that, after ye have done the will of God, ye might receive the promise. For yet a little while, and he that shall come will come, and will not tarry" (Heb. 10:35-37).